For years I have been looking f which would give a thorough i theological and practical aspect people understand why we do 1 issues are. I've just found that book and will be recommending it very widely indeed!
Eddie Arthur, mission blogger and Director for Strategic Initiatives for Global Connections; former Executive Director of Wycliffe Bible Translators

If you want to fire up your church with a vision for global mission, this is your book! It is biblically rich with memorable quotes, and is chock full of inspiring mission stories. The contents page alone is valuable as a sixty-second introduction to a theology of world mission. The book should carry a spiritual health warning, as the local church is challenged about its key role in global mission, and there is the personal challenge of 'where do you fit in God's mission plan?'.
David Coffey OBE, Global Ambassador for BMS World Mission and Past President of the Baptist World Alliance

Easy to read, clear, practical and challenging, this excellent book explores the great story of the mission of the Trinity in Scripture, and gives a thrilling account of how it has been weaved into the story of the Keswick Convention.
John Risbridger, Minister and Team Leader, Above Bar Church, Southampton

Many are telling us that the day of global mission is over: the needs 'at home' are so overwhelming, and the dangers so great, that God cannot want us 'to go' as he did in the past. But God *does* care, and he still wants *us* to care with his compassion for a world of need. I am sure this book will provoke many people to respond to the challenge, as they realize that there are still thousands waiting to be introduced to the Saviour who alone saves and cares.
Dr Helen Roseveare, missionary, speaker and author (1925–2016)

MISSION MATTERS

TIM CHESTER

ivp

MISSION MATTERS

Love Says Go

INTER-VARSITY PRESS
36 Causton Street, London SW1P 4ST, England
Email: ivp@ivpbooks.com
Website: www.ivpbooks.com

British Library Cataloguing-in-Publication Data
A catalogue record for this book is available from the British Library.

ISBN: 978–1–78359–280–7
eBook ISBN: 978–1–78359–282–1

Set in Dante 12/15 pt
Typeset in Great Britain by CRB Associates, Potterhanworth, Lincolnshire
Printed in Great Britain by Ashford Colour Press Ltd, Gosport, Hampshire

Inter-Varsity Press publishes Christian books that are true to the Bible and that communicate the gospel, develop discipleship and strengthen the church for its mission in the world.

IVP originated within the Inter-Varsity Fellowship, now the Universities and Colleges Christian Fellowship, a student movement connecting Christian Unions in universities and colleges throughout Great Britain, and a member movement of the International Fellowship of Evangelical Students. Website: www.uccf.org.uk. That historic association is maintained, and all senior IVP staff and committee members subscribe to the UCCF Basis of Faith.

Contents

Keswick Foundations
Series preface

Our prayer was for deep, clear, powerful teaching,
which would take hold of the souls of the people,
and overwhelm them, and lead them to a full,
definite and all-conquering faith in Jesus.

This simple but profound prayer, expressed by Thomas
Harford-Battersby as he reported on the 1880 Keswick Convention, explains why hundreds of thousands of Christians the
world over have been committed to the Keswick movement.
The *purpose* is nothing other than to see believers more whole-
heartedly committed to Jesus Christ in every area of life,
and the *means* the faithful, clear and relevant exposition of
God's Word.

All around the world, the Keswick movement has this
purpose and this means. Whether it is to proclaim the gospel,
to encourage discipleship, to call for holiness, to urge for
mission, to long for the Spirit's empowering or to appeal for
unity – hearing God's Word in Scripture is central to fulfilling
these priorities. More information about Keswick Ministries
is found at the end of this book.

Keswick Foundations is a series of books which introduce
the priority themes that have shaped the Keswick movement,
themes which we believe continue to be essential for the
church today. By God's grace, for 140 years the movement has

had an impact across the globe, not only through Conventions large and small, but also through a range of media. Books in the Keswick Foundations series provide biblical, accessible and practical introductions to basic evangelical essentials that are vital for every Christian and every local church.

Our prayer for these books is the same as that expressed by Harford-Battersby – that by his Spirit, God's Word will take hold of our souls, leading us to an all-conquering faith in Jesus Christ, which will send us out to live and work for his glory.

Jonathan Lamb
minister-at-large
Keswick Ministries

Foreword

'Mission exists where worship does not,' wrote the author and speaker John Piper.[1] Today, almost 2,000 years after Jesus issued the Great Commission to spread the gospel and disciple the nations, the need for world mission is greater than ever. Mission researchers have identified 16,804 people groups in the world today – ethnic groups with their own sense of identity. And they estimate that 7,289 of these people groups still remain unreached by the gospel, without an indigenous community of believers with the resources to evangelize their own people.[2] This means that over 40% of the world's people groups are still waiting to hear the good news of God's salvation.

The Keswick Convention is passionately committed to responding to this challenge and seeing Christ's Great Commission fulfilled. Indeed, over the years mission has become a foundational element of the Convention's ministry. But Keswick's influence on missions began very humbly in 1885 with a prayer meeting. Interest grew, and in 1887 the Convention held its first official missionary meeting at which Hudson Taylor of OMF (Overseas Missionary Fellowship) was the speaker. Young people wanted to respond to the challenge,

and the Convention realized the role it could play in promoting and channelling individuals into mission. The 'World
Mission Evening' soon became a regular fixture in the
programme, each night seeing between one and four hundred
people respond. In 1938 an astonishing 550 young people
stood to signify their willingness to serve the Lord wherever
he called them.

Over the years the Convention's commitment to mission
has grown, becoming part of the lifeblood of Keswick. History
records the impact this has had. Amy Carmichael, for example,
whose work with the Donahvur Fellowship in India is
renowned, was the first missionary to go out with funding
from the Convention. Similarly, Dr Helen Roseveare, who
worked with WEC International in Zaire (now the Democratic
Republic of Congo) from 1953 to 1973, first heard the call to
missions at Keswick. In her book *Living Faith* she writes about
attending the Convention and the missionary meeting in
1946. 'Unknown to me, I had been waiting for this moment.
Every part of me tingled with fervent joy and happiness
that I was allowed the privilege of responding, and that Christ
was inviting *me* to serve *him*, to be called his ambassador, his
missionary.'[3]

And there are many on the mission field today who could
echo Dr Roseveare's experience and testify to the significance
of the Convention in their own call to mission. Allie Schwaar
remembers attending the Convention for the first time in the
summer of 1996. When David Coffey gave the challenge to
full-time Christian service, she responded. She has been
working with SIM since December 1997 and is now, at
the time of writing, their Communications Manager. She
confesses, 'If you had told me in July 1996 that I would be back
in Keswick in 2006 representing a mission agency, advising
people on mission opportunities and praying for people

responding to God's call on their lives, I would never have believed you! But that's God, isn't it? "He who does immeasurably more than all we ask or imagine, according to his power that is at work within us, to him be the glory." '

Of course, the Convention has had to move with the times and keep up with the changing face of world mission. In the 1990s the Christian Service Centre was introduced to provide information and match people's skills and calling to potential opportunities overseas. In 2002 Earthworks, an interactive exhibition, was developed to challenge people to engage missionally with the world, as well as connect them with individual mission agencies. The emphasis is now no longer exclusively on young people who want to serve in missions, but on believers of all ages and stages of their Christian lives – those nearing retirement and those who want to serve short term.

In 1946 W. H. Aldis, the Keswick Chairman, said at the Convention, 'I suppose the Keswick Convention has done more than any other movement in the Churches to call men and women to the mission field.'4 Today there are many pathways to the mission field, but our prayer is that Keswick will continue to play a significant role in promoting world mission. We pray that the legacy of our commitment to biblical preaching and wholehearted discipleship will be another generation of believers fulfilling the Great Commission wherever God calls.

Elizabeth McQuoid
Trustee of Keswick Ministries
Series Editor of the Keswick Foundations Series
January 2015

Part one:
The God of mission

1

In the love of the Father

Why do mission? Why should you be interested in world mission at all? Why bother to read a book on it? Why is it a foundational value of the Keswick Convention? Why does the Convention dedicate one evening each week to the call to be involved in world mission?

There are many ways in which we could answer the 'Why mission?' question. We could talk about the need to change our broken world and combat injustice. We could talk about the need to rescue people from the judgment of God. We could talk about the command of Christ and his call in the Great Commission to go to the nations.

The Father delights to share his delight in his Son

All of these are good answers. But none of them is the starting point of mission. The starting point is this: *God the Father loves his Son.*

When Jesus was baptized, the voice from heaven said, 'You are my Son, whom I love; with you I am well pleased'

(Luke 3:22). The Father delights in his Son. And because the Father delights in his Son, he delights to share that delight. He loves it when others delight in his Son. The feeling is mutual: the Son delights in his Father and wants to glorify his Father. They rejoice in each other through the Holy Spirit and want to share their joy with others.

This is the starting point of mission. Everything else flows from this. 'Mission' comes from a Latin word that means 'sending'. For the first fifteen centuries or so in the story of the church the word was only ever used to describe what God does. Mission is God sending his Son into the world and sending his Spirit into the world. Our mission is the extension of the mission of the Trinity. And the mission of the Trinity is to share their joy and love.

In John 17:24 Jesus prays, 'Father, I want those you have given me to be with me where I am, and to see my glory, the glory you have given me because you loved me before the creation of the world.' Notice how these statements link together. Jesus wants people to be with him. Why? So they can see the glory that God has given to him. Why? Because God has loved him from before the world began. Mission starts with the Father's love for his Son.

God didn't create the world to meet some need that he had. God wasn't up in heaven on his own feeling lonely. He doesn't need the world. It doesn't add anything to him. God wasn't a frustrated Ruler looking for something to rule. Nor was he a frustrated Creator looking for something to create. He wasn't even a frustrated Lover looking for something to love. He was a Father with a Son living in perfect love through the Spirit. The reason why God created the world and is now redeeming the world is to share his delight in his Son. God created us to be his children, and he recreates us as his children out of the overflow of his love and joy.

At the 2012 Olympics the South African swimmer Chad Le Clos won a gold medal. His father, Bert Le Clos, was famously interviewed afterwards. His joy was uncontained. 'Look at my boy,' he kept saying. 'He's so beautiful.' God the Father creates us so that he could say to us, 'This is my beloved Son in whom I am well pleased.' Mission is God saying through us, 'Look at my Son. He's so beautiful.'

In Proverbs 8 'Wisdom' speaks. It's a reference to Jesus. Jesus, the Wisdom of God, says,

> The LORD brought me forth as the first of his works,
>   before his deeds of old;
> I was formed long ages ago,
>   at the very beginning, when the world came to be.
> (verses 22–23)

When Jesus says he is the 'first of [God's] works', it doesn't mean there was a time before God created Jesus. It's saying that Jesus was eternally begotten before anything else was created.

Wisdom continues,

> Then I was constantly at his side.
> I was filled with delight day after day,
>   rejoicing always in his presence,
> rejoicing in his whole world
>   and delighting in the human race.
> (verses 30–31)

What was Jesus doing before the creation of the world? He was 'filled with delight . . . rejoicing always in [God's] presence'. And what was Jesus doing at the creation of the world? 'Rejoicing in his whole world and delighting in the human race'. Notice the repetition of the words 'delight' and 'rejoice'.

Before creation Jesus delights in God and rejoices in his presence. At creation Jesus delights in those made in God's image and rejoices in God's world. Creation is the overflow of God's joy. Humanity is the overflow of God's delight.

The Son delights in his Father's love and delights to share that love. Both the Father and the Son are out-giving, out-pouring love. And they pour out that love between themselves through the Spirit and out from themselves to others through the Spirit. 'God's love,' says Paul in Romans 5:5, 'has been poured out into our hearts through the Holy Spirit, who has been given to us.' Preaching from John 16, Gottfried Osei-Mensah, the African missionary statesman, told the Keswick Convention, 'The four words, "He shall glorify me", summarise the entire mission of the Holy Spirit . . . And the way he would carry out this work . . . was clearly spelt out: he takes what belongs to Christ and he discloses it to those who belong to Christ.'[1] The persons of the Trinity delight in sharing their love with others and they delight in each receiving love from others.

On the night before he died, Jesus prayed,

> Righteous Father, though the world does not know you, I know you, and they know that you have sent me. I have made you known to them, and will continue to make you known in order that the love you have for me may be in them and that I myself may be in them.
> (John 17:25–26)

Jesus knows the Father and now Jesus has made the Father known to his disciples. Jesus is loved by the Father and now Jesus has made the Father known to us as our Father so that the Father's love may be in us. God wants us to enjoy the love of the trinitarian community and to be part of the trinitarian community. We are united to the Son so that we can be as much part of the divine family as the Son is.

The cascade of divine love

Near where I live is Chatsworth House, one of the finest grand houses in Britain. It's believed to have inspired Pemberley, the house of Darcy, in Jane Austen's novel *Pride and Prejudice* and was used as the location for Pemberley in the 2005 film adaptation of *Pride and Prejudice.* The house and its gardens are open to the public. In the garden is a huge cascading fountain which runs all the way down a hillside in a series of steps. The water flows from one step to another. The public are allowed to paddle in the fountain and walk up the steps.

This is a good image of God's love. The Father is the fountain of life and love, and his life and love fill the Son and overflow through the Son to the world. That love overflows to you, and then through you it keeps on flowing to a needy world.

Where does all the water come from? From the top. It's not that we have to generate love. We don't bring love into existence through an act of will, screwing our faces up to get on with it. All we do is sit under the cascading fountain of the Father's unfailing love, flowing to us from the Father through the Son by the Spirit. We sit there, getting drenched in love, until love flows out from us to a needy world.

We see this cascade of love between the Father and the Son and between the Son and his people in John 17:

- The Father gives words to the Son who gives words to believers:
  'I gave them the words you gave me' (verses 8, 14).

- The Father sends the Son who sends believers:
  'As you sent me into the world, I have sent them into the world' (verse 18).

- The Father is in the Son who is in believers:
  '. . . you are in me and I am in you. May they also be in us . . .' (verse 21).

- The Father gives glory to the Son who gives glory to believers:
  'I have given them the glory that you gave me' (verse 22).

- The Father is one with the Son who is one with believers:
  '. . . that they may be one as we are one' (verse 22).

- The Father is known by the Son who is known by believers:
  'Righteous Father . . . I know you, and . . . I have made you known to them, and will continue to make you known' (verses 25–26).

- The Father loves the Son who loves believers:
  '. . . that the love you have for me may be in them' (verse 26).

What happens when we sit under the fountain of God's love? We become loving people. The apostle John says,

> Everyone who loves has been born of God and knows God. Whoever does not love does not know God, because God is love . . . No one has ever seen God; but if we love one another,

God lives in us and his love is made complete in us . . . We love
because he first loved us.

(1 John 4:7–12, 19)

The cascade of love continues. Those who are loved *by* God
love *like* God.

The sunshine of divine love

The great advantage of this motivation for mission is this: *it
never runs out!*

One of the jokes at the Keswick Convention is that it's easy
to predict the weather: if you can see Skiddaw, the mountain
just to the north of Keswick, then it's going to rain, and if you
can't see it, then it's raining already! Yet even in Keswick when
there's a sunny day, no-one worries that maybe the sun will
run out of light. We don't wander around, full of concern,
saying, 'Much more of this weather and the sun will run out.'
Light and heat just pour out of the sun.

In the same way, love pours out of God in an inexhaustible
stream. God is pouring out life and love. The Father constantly
and continually radiates love to the Son and the Son to the
Father through the Spirit. And God delights for that love to
be shared. It is the Father's great pleasure for the Son to love
others and to be loved by others. It is the Son's great pleasure
for the Father to love others and to be loved by others. This
outpouring of life and love flows out of the Trinity as he
creates the world, loves the world, redeems the world.

Jesus reflects the Father's glory. He is the image of God.
Think of it like a mirror. The light of God's glory is perfectly
reflected in the image or mirror of his Son. The Father sees
in his Son a perfect reflection of his perfections. From all
eternity God's perfections pour out from the Father to the

Son and back to the Father through the Spirit. And this is how we glorify God. It's not that we shine our torches into the sun, saying, 'Here you are, sun. Here's some extra light.' It's not that we sing or work or speak, saying, 'Here you are, God. Here's something extra to add to your perfections.' No, we're mirrors, and when we glorify God, we're reflecting back to God glory that started with him in the first place.

Maybe you have heard people talk about Jesus being *eternally* begotten. This is a way of saying that Jesus has always existed. There was never a moment when he was first created. He is 'begotten' from his Father, but he is eternally begotten. We're used to thinking about what this means for Jesus. But think what this means for the Father. It means he is *eternally* giving life. He is a fountain of life. The Son is eternally loved, and the Father is eternally showing love. He is a fountain of love. Life and love pour out from God.

This motivation for mission is one that can be sustained. Mission is often tough. You may often feel like giving up. You may face opposition and hostility, discouragement and setbacks. You may feel homesick. The people you thought had become Christians may later turn away from Christ. What do we do when these things happen?

We need to go sunbathing! We need to put ourselves again in the sunshine of God's love. The building in which I work is cold. It's an old chapel with thick walls and built into a hillside. So even on a sunny day, we're all wearing several layers. You can feel chilled to the bone. But then you walk out into the sunshine, and the chill starts to dissipate. We live in a cold, graceless world. But when we step into the warmth of God's love, our cold hearts are warmed and our weary souls are energized.

Why should you get involved in world mission? For the same reason that God sent his Son: out of the overflow of divine love.

In 1903 Barclay Buxton, together with his co-worker Paget Wilkes, launched the Japan Evangelistic Band (Nihon Dendo Tai) at the Keswick Convention. Buxton went on to serve in Japan for nearly thirty years. During this time he saw much fruit, but also endured many hardships, including the deaths of two of his daughters. His son writes,

> To him there was but one purpose in view. 'Father, the hour is come; glorify Thy Son' [John 17:1]. He believed each opportunity was God's hour to impart to someone the great salvation procured for us on Calvary. The secret of the blessing which followed his Bible studies lay in a message that was Scriptural, a life that was prayerful and a purpose which was God's glory.[2]

The same purpose inspired Samuel Zwemer, one of the great missionary leaders of the early twentieth century. He was nicknamed 'the Apostle to Islam' because of his work across the Muslim world. He was a missionary for nearly forty years before becoming Professor of Missions at Princeton Theological Seminary. His work was often costly. Like Buxton, he lost two of his daughters. In Zwemer's case, they died, aged four and seven, within eight days of each other. What drove his remarkable missionary endeavour was this vision for the Father's glory in his Son. 'The chief end of missions,' he said, 'is not the salvation of men but the glory of God.'[3] 'God has created the entire world that it should be the theatre of his glory by the spread of his Gospel.'[4] Zwemer visited the Keswick Convention on a number of occasions. In 1923 he closed his address to the Convention with a paraphrase of the prayer of Jesus in John 17: 'Father, the hour has come; glorify thy Son in the Islamic world that thy Son may also glorify thee in the Islamic world!'[5]

2

In the name of the Son[1]

> We live in a situation of conflict today in which Christians are
> called upon to express who we are, what we believe and why
> our faith matters in the midst of all sorts of other rival claims
> and conflicting loyalties – whether those are of other religious
> faiths, resurgent atheism, or just sheer apathy. As in the days of
> the apostles, so today there are those who reject Jesus and any
> claim that he is the Lord . . . So knowing the living God is a
> privilege God has entrusted to us, and then the responsibility
> of making him known in the midst of competing claims in
> the world.[2]

So said Chris Wright, the International Ministries Director of
the Langham Partnership, at the Keswick Convention in 2011.

We live in a pluralistic world – a world of many 'competing
claims'. One of the great challenges of world mission is
finding yourself a minority in a nation where the majority
follow another religion. Even in the West the world is now on
our doorstep. Perhaps a third of the people who lived on my
road in Sheffield were Muslim. The best-attended place of

worship in my area was the mosque. There were over a hundred nationalities in my former neighbourhood and a huge variety of beliefs. One hundred years ago if someone said in my neighbourhood, 'Follow God', it would have meant only one thing: become a Christian, put your faith in Christ, join the church. Not any more. Even in areas where there isn't a large immigrant population, there is a wide variety of beliefs: atheists, agnostics, New Age.

Imagine you're lying in bed at night asleep. Suddenly you hear a loud knocking and a stranger shouting, 'Let me in, in the name of John Smith.' You might be inclined to shout back, 'Who are you? Go away. Don't you realize what time it is?' But if you could see that it was a police officer and he was shouting, 'Open up in the name of the law', then you would open up straight away. He is acting with the authority of the State, and that makes all the difference. Someone who knocks on doors in the middle of the night is a social nuisance. A police officer who knocks on doors, by contrast, is a public servant. That's because he acts in the name of the law. That name, that title, conveys authority.

Or what if someone called Mr Jones asks you to change your life? Why would you listen? But what about someone called *Doctor* Jones? If a doctor is telling you to eat less fatty food, then you're likely to listen. It's all in the name, and the authority it conveys.

So what about a friend who says, 'Repent and believe the good news'? People are *unlikely to listen* to our message unless they have some sense of the name in which we speak. I would suggest, too, that we're *unlikely to speak* our message unless we have some sense of the name in which we speak.

The gospel is a big ask. When you share the gospel, you're asking people to change their whole lives. You are saying in effect, 'You shouldn't be in charge of your life; God should be in charge of your life.' Jesus' 'evangelistic pitch' was: 'If you want to follow me, take up your cross.' Come and die. Follow Jesus and you might get martyred. Even if you don't get martyred, you must die to self. If you're going to tell people to change their whole lives, you need to be confident you've got the authority to do that. I sometimes say, 'If there's one thing worse for a preacher than having people ignore him, it's having people listen to him!' People sometimes say to me, 'I heard you speak once and then I did this.' It's a scary moment – I'm not sure I want to be responsible for people changing the direction of their lives! We need to be confident in the authority of what we're saying. Or think about some of the specifics. In your evangelism you might say, 'Following Jesus means you've got to stop sleeping with your partner.' 'Following Jesus means you've got to write some big cheques because God calls you to generosity.' Are you going to say that?

'What gives you the right to preach at me?' 'Why should I listen to you?' 'By what authority?' 'In whose name?' That's what the religious leaders ask in Acts 4:7: 'By what power or what name did you do this?' It won't surprise you if I tell you the answer is: Jesus. We do mission in the name of Jesus. The question, then, is: 'What's so special about the name of Jesus?'

Why does the name of Jesus convey authority?

1. Jesus is the Saviour who alone can save

One afternoon Peter and John, two of the apostles, healed a lame man outside the temple in Jerusalem. Then the man went into the temple, leaping and praising God. People began to realize that this man was the beggar they'd often seen at the gate. You can imagine them saying, 'That crazy man looks a bit like the beggar . . . Wait a minute, he *is* the beggar!' So they were astounded. They gathered round the man who was now holding tightly to Peter and John. Peter saw his opportunity and addressed the crowd.

'Why does this surprise you?' he begins (perhaps a rather redundant question!). 'Why do you stare at us as if by our own power or godliness we had made this man walk?' In other words, it's not our power. It's not in our name. God has done this to glorify Jesus: 'By faith in the name of Jesus, this man whom you see and know was made strong. It is Jesus' name and the faith that comes through him that has completely healed him, as you can all see' (Acts 3:16). Twice Peter says it is by faith in the name of Jesus.

It's not that his name is magical. You can't go 'Jesus, Jesus, Jesus' and make some miracle occur. His name represents or summarizes who he is and what he's done. Peter explains by telling the story of Jesus. Jesus is the One promised by God, the One whom you killed, the One whom God raised, the One who will return to restore all things. There is power and life and hope in the name of Jesus because of what he has accomplished through his death and resurrection.

While Peter and John were speaking, the temple guard arrived. The temple leaders were disturbed because Peter and John had said that Jesus had risen from the dead. Peter and John were put in prison overnight. Then the next day Peter and John were brought before the Jewish council. 'By what power or what name did you do this?' they asked.

Peter begins his response by saying, 'If we are being called to account today for an act of kindness shown to a man who was lame and are being asked how he was *healed*, then know this . . .' (4:9–10, italics added). The word 'healed' is actually the word 'saved' (Peter uses a different word in 3:16). It's a provocative word to use. In one sense he's just saying that this man was saved from his disability. But this is the

Jewish council. They knew that when the day of God's salvation came, the lame would leap for joy. Isaiah 35:6 promised,

> Then will the lame leap like a deer,
>   and the mute tongue shout for joy.

And that's what Luke describes in Acts 3:8: The lame man is leaping and praising God.

So Peter is saying that the day of salvation has arrived, right here, right now, in the middle of history. God's kingdom has come and it has come through Jesus. This healing is a sign of the beginning of the new age. In other words, this is not *just* a healing. (Hospitals and other religions do healings.) This is a sign of salvation. And it's a sign that salvation is found in the name of Jesus. The Jewish leaders thought that when the kingdom of God dawned, they would be at the heart of it. But Peter is saying that this healing is a sign that the day of salvation has dawned and it has bypassed them.

Peter continues, 'It is by the name of Jesus Christ of Nazareth, whom you crucified but whom God raised from the dead, that this man stands before you healed' (4:10). This is a surprise. Not perhaps to us who know the story well. But it would have been scandalous for Peter's hearers. A crucified Saviour? It's still shocking today. A Saviour whose great, defining act is to die? What's saving about that? No-one gets healed on Good Friday. No-one is liberated. There is just agony and pain and darkness.

When Jesus hung on the cross, 'the chief priests and the teachers of the law mocked him among themselves. "He saved others," they said, "but he can't save himself!"' (Mark 15:31). Peter now stands before those very same people and says, 'Salvation is found in the name of the *crucified* Jesus.' 'He saved others, but he can't save himself,' they said. The truth is that he saves others *because* he did not save himself. He saves *through* his death. He carries our sin and our punishment in our place.

Jesus was not only crucified, but 'God raised [him] from the dead' (Acts 4:10). No other religious figure has risen from the dead. This is what makes Jesus unique:

- He saves through sacrifice, through his death.
- He has risen from the dead.

Peter concludes, 'Salvation is found in no one else, for there is no other name under heaven given to mankind by which we must be saved' (4:12). No-one else. No other name. Peter is alluding to two or three passages from the Old Testament, one of which is Isaiah 45:21–23:

> And there is no God apart from me,
> a righteous God and a Saviour;
>   there is none but me.
> 'Turn to me and be saved,
>   all you ends of the earth;
>   for I am God, and there is no other.
> By myself I have sworn,
>   my mouth has uttered in all integrity
>   a word that will not be revoked:
> before me every knee will bow;
>   by me every tongue will swear.'

Notice what these verses claim: 'There is no God apart from me.' 'There is no . . . Saviour . . . but me.' 'I am God, and there is no other.' Peter takes this great statement of monotheism, the belief that there is only one God, and says that it's talking about Jesus. There is one God and one Saviour, he says – and his name is Jesus.

The true God is not the god of philosophy or religion. We must not assume what God is like and then ask whether Jesus fits the description. We must allow Jesus and his cross to redefine our notions of God. God is not some impersonal ultimate Absolute, nor a deistic god who looks on his world with indifference, nor a god who must be placated through religious duties, nor is he a lenient god who indulgently overlooks our rebellion and the suffering it causes. He is the God of the cross: the God who offered himself in love to reconcile us to himself.

Is it arrogant for us to say Jesus is the only name?
But surely it's arrogant to claim Jesus is the only way? There's a traditional story called 'The Blind Men and the Elephant' which was written as a poem in the nineteenth century by John Godfrey Saxe. It begins:

> It was six men of Indostan
> To learning much inclined,
> Who went to see the Elephant
> (Though all of them were blind),
> That each by observation
> Might satisfy his mind.

The first blind man feels the stomach of the elephant and concludes it's a wall. The second feels the trunk and concludes it's a snake. The rest conclude it's a spear, tree, fan and rope, depending upon where they touch. Saxe's conclusion is:

> So oft in theologic wars,
> The disputants, I ween,

Rail on in utter ignorance
Of what each other mean,
And prate about an Elephant
Not one of them has seen!

What the story purports to show is that all religions are blind attempts to understand ultimate reality. All religions reflect the truth, but none grasps the whole truth.

But the real question is: How do you know it's an elephant? How do you know it's not a wall and that five of the blind men are wrong? The story actually reveals the arrogance of the pluralists or relativists. They claim to be the sighted ones in a world of blind men. They claim they know the truth towards which others can only partly, blindly stumble. It's the pluralists who arrogantly claim that they alone know the truth.

It's arrogant to claim that Christianity is the only true religion *if* by that we mean that we have worked it out, that Christians are the clever ones. But that is not what we are claiming. Religion is:

- human beings trying to know the ultimate reality (however that is defined)
- human beings trying to be saved (however that is defined)

Religion in its various forms is the account of human spiritual longings, searching, efforts, rituals. Religions purport to tell us how we can reach up to God.

But the message of Jesus is the exact opposite. It is the story of God reaching down to us by sending his Son, Jesus. Jesus is God showing us God and reconciling us to God.

The gospel is not an arrogant claim that we and we alone have worked out the truth about God, that we and we alone have achieved goodness and perfection. It's the humble claim that we are ignorant people who have received God's revelation in Jesus, and that we are wicked people who have received God's reconciliation in Jesus. The message of Jesus is not about what we do to reach up to heaven, but how God has come down from heaven.

- We proclaim it confidently because it's from God;
- We proclaim it humbly because it's not from us.

In 2011 Chris Wright told the Keswick Convention,

> What we are claiming is nothing to do with ourselves. It is not about how wonderful Christians are, how great a religion we have, and the answers we have come up with for the world's problems. No, it is not a claim about ourselves, it is simply a witness and a testimony to what the Scriptures – the Old and New Testament – tell us about the one true living God and how, and where, and through whom this living God has acted in order to bring salvation to us and to the whole of creation.[3]

Is it cruel for God to say Jesus is the only name?
Or is it callous of God to say that Jesus is the only name? That's what I heard someone say recently. If people say to God, 'I followed you through Hinduism' or 'I followed your through Islam', and he replies, 'You made the wrong choice, so off you go to hell', then that would be cruel and arbitrary. Who would want to worship a god like that?

But let me tell you what I think is cruel: a God who sends his only beloved Son to endure the cross to save people when they could be saved another way. Imagine a God who sends his only Son to this world, and his Son sweats blood at the prospect of the cross and cries out in anguish, 'My Father, if it is possible, may this cup be taken from me. Yet not as I will, but as you will' (Matthew 26:39). And this god replies, 'There is another way. There are many ways by which people can be saved. But still I'm going to send you to the cross. For no good reason.' That is what would be cruel. That is not a god that I could worship.

The point is that there is no other way. All the insights of religion and all the efforts of religion, however well intentioned and earnest they may be, cannot save us. Isaac Watts puts it like this:

Not all the blood of beasts
On Jewish altars slain
Could give the guilty conscience peace
Or wash away the stain.

But Christ, the heav'nly Lamb,
Takes all our sins away;
A sacrifice of nobler name
And richer blood than they.[4]

The cross is the great demonstration that there is no other name and no other way, because if there were another way, the Father would not have sent his beloved Son to die.

There is no other way, but this way is all-sufficient. There's a sense in which our message is *exclusive*, 'for there is no other name under heaven given to mankind by which we must be saved' (Acts 4:12). No-one else. No other name. Yet at the same time, it's the most *inclusive* of messages. This name has been given to all people. It saves – whoever you are, wherever you're from, whatever you've done.

2. Jesus is the Saviour whom we must proclaim

Jesus is the only name that saves. But that's not an easy thing to say today. People think it sounds arrogant or cruel. It grates in our pluralistic culture.

There's nothing new in that. After Peter's speech, the Jewish leaders nevertheless command the disciples 'not to speak or teach at all in the name of Jesus' (4:17–18; 5:28, 40–41). They say, in effect, as people say to us today, that you can be religious as long as you don't proclaim Jesus as the *only* Saviour. The culture in which Peter and John lived didn't want to hear the name of Jesus. And neither does ours today.

Peter and John's response is this: 'Which is right in God's eyes: to listen to you, or to him? You be the judges! As for us, we cannot help speaking about what we have seen and heard' (Acts 4:19–20). Are we going to fit into our culture or are we going to obey God? Chris Wright says, 'Either Jesus is the only Saviour and Lord of the world or he is not. If he is, then . . . we are called to stand up for him with loyalty and unwavering witness, no matter what the hostility, the enmity, the persecution or just sheer apathy of the world around us.'[5]

It's all too easy for us to talk 'around' Jesus – to talk about our church or our social projects – but not to talk about Jesus himself. In conversations with our friends we need to name the name of Jesus.

It's not easy. The first Christians didn't find it easy either. So when Peter and John are told not to speak in the name of Jesus, they go home and pray with the other disciples. We can't do it on our own, but we can do it in the power of the Holy Spirit. This is what those first Christians prayed: 'Now, Lord, consider their threats and enable your servants to speak your word with great boldness' (Acts 4:29). And as a result of that prayer, 'they were all filled with the Holy Spirit and spoke the word of God boldly' (4:31).

3

In the power of the Spirit[1]

At the beginning of Acts Jesus tells his disciples, 'Do not leave Jerusalem, but wait for the gift my Father promised, which you have heard me speak about. For John baptised with water, but in a few days you will be baptised with the Holy Spirit' (Acts 1:4–5). In effect, he is saying, 'Don't do anything until you've received the Holy Spirit.'

Luke has just talked about Jesus 'giving instructions through the Holy Spirit' (Acts 1:2). Think about this for a moment. Jesus gave instructions 'through the Holy Spirit'. What does that mean? Did Jesus, the Son of God, the risen Lord, need the Holy Spirit? Apparently he did. He conducted his mission from beginning to end in the power of the Holy Spirit (Acts 10:38).

And now he gives that same Spirit to us today. This is how we will do the mission Jesus has given to us. He says in Acts 1:8, 'You will receive power when the Holy Spirit comes on you; and you will be my witnesses in Jerusalem, and in all Judea and Samaria, and to the ends of the earth.' This is what happens. All the way through the book of Acts people receive the Holy Spirit when they become Christians, and so they are empowered for mission. The Holy Spirit empowers and directs the mission of God's people.

In its early days the Keswick Convention was associated with a view that, if Christians surrendered themselves, they could experience the Holy Spirit in a way that leads to a 'higher life' of greater victory over sin. Although this two-stage view of the Christian life is no longer taught, the emphasis on living and working in the power of the Spirit remains. The Convention seeks 'to encourage a dependency upon the indwelling and fullness of the Holy Spirit for life transformation and effective living'. Back in 1895 Andrew Murray, the South African mission leader, told the Keswick Convention,

> If we are to be real Missionaries, if we are to give our money as we ought to give, and give ourselves and our children, and pray as we ought to pray, and live as we ought to live, we must have nothing less than the power of the Holy Spirit flowing freely in us to overflowing. Oh, Keswick, thou canst not do the right mission work unless the Holy Spirit fill every heart. O Christ, we want to live and die like Thee, for God's Kingdom! Give Thine own Spirit within us.[2]

Andrew Murray first visited the Convention while convalescing from a throat problem. There he met a young man named Spencer Walton whom he encouraged to come as a missionary to South Africa. Together they went on to form what in time became the Africa Evangelical Fellowship (now part of SIM).

Here are six things that the Spirit does in the book of Acts. My aim is to raise our expectations and fuel our prayers. Why don't we see these same things happening today? Perhaps it's because we don't expect them and because we don't pray for them.

Six things that the Holy Spirit does in Acts

1. The Spirit directs the mission of God's people

The Holy Spirit is the great Mission Director. Consider how the story of Acts unfolds. In one sense the plan is revealed at the beginning: 'But you will receive power when the Holy Spirit comes on you; and you will be my witnesses in Jerusalem, and in all Judea and Samaria, and to the ends of the earth' (Acts 1:8).

But notice how the gospel makes the move from Jerusalem to Judea and Samaria: 'On that day a great persecution broke out against the church in Jerusalem, and all except the apostles were scattered throughout Judea and Samaria . . . Those who had been scattered preached the word wherever they went' (Acts 8:1–4). The next stage of the plan didn't happen at the initiative of the apostles. In fact, it wasn't part of their plan at all. It happened at God's initiative. And it happened through the strangest of means – a great persecution.

In Acts 11:19–23 we see the gospel taking the next step, moving from Judea and Samaria to the Gentiles. Again it's persecution that drives the gospel outwards. And again the apostles didn't plan it, authorize it or even *know* about it! They only discovered what was happening *after* the event. The book of Acts is not the story of the apostles making plans and then putting them into effect. It's the story of the Holy Spirit directing mission.

We don't need a call to mission. We already have one – the Great Commission. But sometimes the Spirit prompts a church, as he does in Acts 13:1–3, to send their best people. Or he gives an individual a specific prompt to leave home to proclaim Christ in new cultures. And the Keswick World Mission Evening has often been the occasion for this.

In Acts 16 Paul and his companions plan to go to the province of Asia (part of modern-day Turkey), but they go to Phrygia and Galatia instead, 'having been kept by the Holy Spirit from preaching the word in the province of Asia' (verse 6). What does that mean? We don't actually know. It may have been a dream or a vision. It may have been circumstances. Then they plan to go to Bithynia (in northern Turkey), but they go to Mysia and Troas instead. Why don't they go to Bithynia? 'The Spirit of Jesus would not allow them to' (verse 7). Then Paul sees a vision of a man from Macedonia asking them to help. So they travel to Macedonia. Macedonia is in Greece. This is the first time the gospel enters Europe. Whose plan was that? It wasn't Paul's. Paul would have been in the province of Asia if he'd had his way. Or if not Asia, then Bithynia. No, this was the Holy Spirit's plan!

Think about what's going on here. Imagine that you send out missionaries from your church to Turkey. Your church agrees that this is your vision. You assess their suitability for work in Turkey. You share your vision with others. You publicize your plans. You hold a meeting to commission them and send them off. And then the first prayer letter you get home says, 'By the way, the Spirit of Jesus prevented us from preaching in Turkey, so we're in Greece instead.' That's what has just happened with Paul and his companions.

The Holy Spirit is the great mission strategist. And this is good news. The burden of planning mission is lifted from us. This doesn't mean we can switch our brains off. We still have to make decisions which need to be thought through and informed. But I can trust God to use my small contributions as part of his big mission plan. So we can be faithful and let the Spirit coordinate his mission to the world.

2. The Spirit creates opportunities to speak of Jesus

The direction of the Spirit is not only true of the big picture. It's also true of day-to-day opportunities. At one point in the story of Acts an angel tells Philip to go to the Gaza road (Acts 8:26–31). There Philip sees the chariot of an Ethiopian official, and the Spirit says to Philip, 'Go to that chariot.' Philip discovers the Ethiopian is reading the Bible and he asks, 'Do you understand what you are reading?' The Ethiopian replies, 'How can I . . . unless someone explains it to me?' So Philip explains the gospel, and the official is baptized and takes the gospel back to Ethiopia.

Imagine the Spirit tells you to go to a café, and when you get there, the Spirit says, 'Sit at that table.' And you notice that the person at the next table is reading the Bible. So you say, 'Do you understand what you're reading?' At the end of the conversation they say, 'Can I be baptized?' Or the Spirit says, 'Go to the Penrith Road.' And then the Spirit says, 'Hitch a lift in that car.' And you notice a Bible on the back seat. So you say, 'Do you understand what you're reading?' Do you have that expectation of the Spirit's work? Do you pray for this kind of Spirit-led opportunity today?

Soon after, in the story of Acts, a man called Cornelius who longs to know God is given a vision and told to send people to find Simon Peter, one of the apostles. Meanwhile, Peter sees a vision. We read, 'While Peter was still thinking about the vision, the Spirit said to him, "Simon, three men are looking for you. So get up and go downstairs. Do not hesitate to go with them, for I have sent them"' (Acts 10:19–20).

The Spirit tells Peter to go with these men. And not only does the Spirit bring Christians to unbelievers, but he brings unbelievers to Christians. The Spirit says, 'Do not hesitate to go with them, for I have sent them.' The Spirit is working in the lives of unbelievers, preparing them to hear the gospel and bringing them into contact with Christians. Philip Hacking, former Chair of the Keswick Convention, says, 'The same Lord who moves us to take good news will be moving at the other end in the lives of people to receive it.'[3]

When the first missionaries rowed ashore off the coast of Liberia, they were met by an excited African man. 'I know who you are,' he said. 'You are missionaries! God appeared to me in a dream and told me to come to the coast and meet people who would preach good news to my tribe.'[4]

I remember hearing the story of a Christian couple in Iran. They were making a long journey, so they committed to share the gospel with someone each day. Towards the end of one day they went to buy petrol, and at the petrol station there was a man with a full beard and a gun, a sign that he was a radical Muslim. The wife said, 'I think you should tell that man the gospel.' But the husband said, 'Are you joking? Do you want me to get killed?' And he drove off. But his wife kept on at him. 'We said we would share the gospel with someone every day . . . I think God was leading us to that man . . .' In the end, the husband slammed on the brakes and turned the car round. 'OK,' he said, 'if you're determined to be a widow, I'll talk to him.' So he went up to the man and said, 'Do you want to know God?' At this, the man started crying. Three days before he had had a dream that told him to wait in that spot at that time and someone would tell him how he could know God.

Why doesn't this sort of thing happen to me? Perhaps because I don't expect it and because I don't pray for it.

3. The Spirit gives faith when people hear God's word

Peter goes with the men sent by Cornelius. Cornelius gathers all his family and friends. So Peter finds himself proclaiming the gospel to a 'large gathering' (10:24–27). We read, 'While

Peter was still speaking these words, the Holy Spirit came on all who heard the message. The circumcised believers who had come with Peter were astonished that the gift of the Holy Spirit had been poured out even on Gentiles' (Acts 10:44–45; see also 11:15–16; 15:8).

When H. B. Garlock arrived in Liberia in 1920, he opened a school. King Jufuli, the king of the region, sent his son there. One morning they were reading the story of Jesus healing blind Bartimaeus. The son had cataracts, so he asked if Jesus could heal his blindness. Garlock hesitated before inviting the boy to pray and believe. As they prayed together, the cataracts completely disappeared. The boy immediately ran to his father to show him what had happened. Here was proof that Jesus was alive. The news spread rapidly, and many put their faith in Jesus, including the king himself.[5]

Recently we got to know one of my wife's colleagues. She loved hanging out with our gospel community. But she found the gospel message weird! We did some Bible studies with her, and she kept looking at us in astonishment. Walking on water, rising from the dead, ascending into heaven. 'You believe all of that stuff?' she asked. Later she told us that we seemed like sensible people who were holding down jobs, but we believed all this crazy, wacky stuff. But then she described a moment while sitting on the floor in her front room when suddenly she knew it was all true. What happened in that moment? The Holy Spirit came on her. The Holy Spirit gave her faith in Jesus.

Why doesn't this sort of thing happen more often? Perhaps because I don't expect it and because I don't pray for it.

4. *The Spirit empowers God's people to speak God's word*
In Acts 3 – 4 Peter and John heal a lame man outside the temple, as we saw in the last chapter. When they proclaim

the message of Jesus to the crowd that gathers, they are thrown into prison and then brought before the religious leaders. This was an intimidating moment for Peter and John. But we are told that Peter addressed them 'filled with the Holy Spirit' (Acts 4:8), bravely affirming that salvation is found in no-one other than Jesus. When the religious leaders saw the courage of these 'unschooled, ordinary men, they were astonished' (Acts 4:13). Peter is an ordinary guy with no education, but he is filled with the Holy Spirit, and people are astonished at his courage. We are not given a task which matches our powers. We are given a power (the Holy Spirit) which matches our task (winning the nations).

The religious leaders command Peter and John to stop evangelizing. But Peter says, 'Which is right in God's eyes: to listen to you, or to him? You be the judges! As for us, we cannot help speaking about what we have seen and heard' (Acts 4:19–20).

The religious leaders threaten and then release them. Peter and John go back to the church, and the church 'raised their voices together in prayer to God' (Acts 4:24–30). This is the first time that the church has been threatened. So what do they pray? They don't pray for an end to opposition. In fact, they affirm that opposition is part of God's plan. Instead, they pray for boldness and miracles. Why that combination of boldness and miracles? Because the last time God performed a miracle, two Christians got thrown into prison. It's almost as if they are saying, 'Father, if you're going to go around performing miracles, you had better give us boldness, because your miracles get us into trouble!' And this is what happens: 'After they prayed, the place where they were meeting was shaken. And they were all filled with the Holy Spirit and spoke the word of God boldly' (Acts 4:31).

What happens when you pray for boldness? God fills you with his Spirit.

What happens when God fills you with his Spirit? You proclaim the word of God with boldness.

Why don't I proclaim God's word with boldness? Perhaps because I don't expect it and because I don't pray for it.

5. The Spirit confounds opposition to God's word

Later in the story of Acts, Paul and Barnabas come to the island of Cyprus where they get the opportunity to preach to the Governor. But a sorcerer called Elymas 'opposed them and tried to turn the proconsul from the faith' (Acts 13:8). Paul is filled with the Holy Spirit, looks straight at Elymas and says, ' "You are a child of the devil and an enemy of everything that is right . . . Now the hand of the Lord is against you. You are going to be blind . . ." Immediately mist and darkness came over him', and he has to be led away (Acts 13:10–11).

H. B. Garlock, a missionary to Liberia, once went to a tribe to rescue a kidnapped girl when he found himself surrounded by a mob. Garlock wrote,

> They made a mad rush toward me with drawn knives, shouting, 'Kill him, kill him!' The leader rushed at me with his cutlass raised to behead me . . . I closed my eyes and committed myself to God, repeating over and over again that one name that is above every name, 'Jesus, Jesus!' Suddenly, there was a deathlike stillness! The tom-toms stopped beating and all screaming and yelling halted abruptly . . . I cautiously opened my eyes – and wondered if I could believe them. Before me stood some of the savages with their weapons upraised ready to strike, while others held drawn knives at their sides. But all were frozen in their tracks . . . The God that closed the lions' mouths in Daniel's times had held these wild, angry cannibals at bay! I have often wondered if they saw the

Angel of the Lord . . . Or perhaps . . . they saw the horses and chariots of fire encircling our little company. One thing was certain – they did feel and see something that caused them to know that God was there protecting his servants. God had performed a miracle before our very eyes.[6]

Samuel Zwemer, the so-called 'Apostle to Islam' whom we met in the last chapter, wrote many booklets introducing Muslims to the message of Jesus. On one occasion a Muslim teacher ripped one into small pieces before his class. Intrigued by a message that provoked such anger, one of the students gathered up the fragments and pieced it together. What he read led to his conversion.

In Acts 6 we're told the story of Stephen. He too performs miraculous signs that bring him into conflict with the members of the synagogue. But, we're told, 'they could not stand up against the wisdom the Spirit gave him as he spoke' (Acts 6:10).

Imagine. When your school friends laugh at you, or the colleague in the office argues with you, or people belittle your faith or pull holes in what you say, imagine the Spirit speaking through you in a way that no-one can refute.

Why am I unable to confound those who reject and ridicule God's word? Perhaps because I don't expect it and because I don't pray for it.

6. The Spirit gives comfort and joy to God's people

Stephen is brought before the religious council. He bravely proclaims the gospel, and they respond with fury, gnashing their teeth at him – they're in a frenzy! And we read, 'But Stephen, full of the Holy Spirit, looked up to heaven and saw the glory of God, and Jesus standing at the right hand of God' (Acts 7:55).

What a moment! God doesn't rescue Stephen from the fury of the crowd. Stephen is stoned to death because God gets so much glory through the faithful suffering of his servant. But in God's kindness, the Holy Spirit gives Stephen a vision of the glory that is waiting for him.

Soon after this, Luke says, 'The church throughout Judea, Galilee and Samaria enjoyed a time of peace and was strengthened. Living in the fear of the Lord and encouraged by the Holy Spirit, it increased in numbers' (Acts 9:31). And in Acts 13:52 he writes, 'And the disciples were filled with joy and with the Holy Spirit.'

Why am I not filled with joy? Why are the people in my church struggling to find joy amid the pressures of motherhood or their work situation? Why don't our hearts rise above our circumstances to stand with Jesus in the presence of the Father? Perhaps *they* struggle to find Spirit-inspired joy because *I* don't expect it and because I don't pray for it.

The Holy Spirit is the great missionary, working in all these different ways to bring glory to Jesus. I'm sure you have some experience of seeing such things happen. But why don't we see them happening more? I don't know the answer to that question. But perhaps one reason is that we don't expect them to happen, so we don't pray for them to happen.

The reality is that all too often I think my contribution counts for more than God's. I know it sounds ridiculous, but often that's our attitude. We think that what *we* do is what really matters. Now God could reach the world without us, but he graciously involves us. So our actions do matter, our words do matter, our witness does matter. But we flip it round. Instead of this being God's mission in which he invites us to participate, we think it's our mission and God can help us if he wants. Yet Jesus himself said, 'Apart from me you can do nothing' (John 15:5).

The Spirit empowers us for mission. That's a great encouragement to do mission. Peter Maiden, former Chair of Keswick Convention and former International Director of Operation Mobilisation, told the Convention,

> The church, transformed by the Spirit, is immediately thrust out in witness . . . There is work to be done. It is a work of the Holy Spirit but it's a work in which the Holy Spirit will involve the church, and his intention is to involve every church member, every believer. It's the work of taking this glorious gospel to the people of the world.[7]

Part two:
The story of mission

4

A promise for the nations

Suppose you were asked to give a talk on world mission. What Bible text would you use? There are, of course, many good options. Mission permeates the pages of the New Testament.

But when Paul wants to defend his mission to the Gentiles, he turns to the promise to Abraham in the Old Testament. He's following the lead of Jesus. On the first Easter Day Jesus turns to the Old Testament to show that the proclamation of repentance and forgiveness to the nations has always been part of God's plan (Luke 24:44–47). The missionary text of the New Testament church was not the Great Commission in Matthew 28, but the Old Testament.

In this chapter we'll see how mission is central to the message of the Old Testament, and in the next we'll turn to the New Testament.

Created with a mission

The Bible story starts with God making man and woman to know him and reflect his glory. He tells us, 'Be fruitful and increase in number; fill the earth and subdue it' (Genesis 1:28). We are given a mission: to fill the earth and rule over the earth. God makes us *in his image* (Genesis 1:27). It's the language used of idolatry. In Daniel 3 King Nebuchadnezzar sets up an 'image' of himself before which all people must bow. It represents his power and glory. The *true* God, the living God, is represented by us! God placed humanity in his world to reflect his glory: our mission is to rule over God's world to the glory of God.

A twisted mission

After our rebellion against God, humanity's mission warps and twists. The story of Babel is a graphic sign of this (Genesis 11). Instead of spreading out to fill the earth, humanity comes together. Instead of living for the glory of God, they build a tower to make a name for themselves. We're still on a mission, but now that mission is self-centred.

The world is full of people with drive and purpose. They may want to make money or build a career or have a successful family or create a beautiful home or secure their future. But that drive and purpose is no longer for God's glory. Many modern companies have mission statements, but that mission is no longer centred on God.

A promise for the nations

It's in the context of this self-centred mission that God makes his promises to Abraham. He changes Abraham's name from 'Abram', which means 'exalted father', to 'Abraham', which means 'father of a multitude' (Genesis 17:4–6).

The choice of Abraham is the point in the story where God focuses down on one person and one family. But right from the beginning God says that his purposes for Abraham and Israel are for the sake of the nations:

- 'I will bless those who bless you,
    and whoever curses you I will curse;
  and all peoples on earth
    will be blessed through you.'
  (Genesis 12:3)

- 'Abraham will surely become a great and powerful nation,
  and all nations on earth will be blessed through him.'
  (Genesis 18:18)

The hope of the nations is found in one family and one nation – and nowhere else. But this family is the hope of the nation. Abraham is not chosen *instead of* the nations, but *for* the nations.

This is how Paul defends his mission to the Gentiles or nations:

Scripture foresaw that God would justify the Gentiles
by faith, and announced the gospel in advance to Abraham:
'All nations will be blessed through you' . . . If you belong to
Christ, then you are Abraham's seed, and heirs according
to the promise.
(Galatians 3:8, 29)

The word 'Gentiles' in the New Testament can just as well be translated 'nations'. (The Gentiles were all the nations who weren't Jewish.) So Paul is saying that the promise to Abraham that God would bless the nations was the gospel announced in advance. This promise is now being fulfilled through his proclamation of Christ to the nations. This is his mandate for mission. This is what he turns to when he wants to justify his mission to the Gentiles (Romans 1:1–6; 9:24–29; 16:25–27; Ephesians 3:1–6).

We see Abraham rescuing nations (Genesis 14) and interceding for nations (Genesis 18:22–33). But we also see him failing in his calling. Shortly after receiving the promise that he will be a blessing to the nations, Abraham lies to the king of Egypt about Sarai. So the king takes Sarai into his household, with the result that 'the LORD inflicted serious diseases on Pharaoh and his household' (Genesis 12:17). God has chosen Abraham to bless all nations, but Abraham will only do this as he directs his family in the ways of the Lord (Genesis 18:18–19).

A light to the nations

Abraham's family becomes the nation of Israel. At Mount Sinai, after he has rescued them through the exodus, God makes them his people through a covenant. This covenant reaffirms and clarifies their missionary calling. Philip Hacking once told the Convention, 'Just as Abraham was called out of the world to go back into it as a man with the blessings of God, so the people of God were called out of Egypt to become a nation to serve the world.'[1] This is how God introduces the covenant:

> You yourselves have seen what I did to Egypt, and how I carried you on eagles' wings and brought you to myself. Now if you obey me fully and keep my covenant, then out of all nations you will be my treasured possession. Although the whole earth is mine, you will be for me a kingdom of priests and a holy nation.
> (Exodus 19:4–6)

In Israel the priests taught the law and offered sacrifices of atonement so that the people could come to God. Here God calls on Israel to be a priestly kingdom in the midst of the nations. The nation as a whole is to take the knowledge of God to the nations and bring the nations to the means of atonement with God. 'Holy' means 'set apart', so to be a holy nation was to be a distinctive nation among the nations. Israel was to reflect the holiness of God. They were to 'be holy because I, the LORD your God, am holy' (Leviticus 19:2). By reflecting the holiness of God in a distinctive way, they would make him known to the nations. So a key purpose of the law was to help Israel to be missional. It defined what it meant for Israel to be a priestly kingdom and a holy nation who would make God known to the nations and bring the nations to God through atonement. 'The true missionary concept of the Old Testament,' says Philip Hacking, 'lay in a desire to spread the knowledge of God and his ways and also to demonstrate the attractive otherness of the people of God. In this way, holiness and outreach went hand in hand.'[2]

Often at weddings, ministers use the blessing of Aaron:

The LORD bless you
    and keep you;
the LORD make his face shine on you
    and be gracious to you;
the LORD turn his face towards you
    and give you peace.
(Numbers 6:24–26)

God tells us the significance of this blessing: 'So they will put my name upon the Israelites, and I will bless them' (verse 27). By this prayer, God marks out Israel as his chosen nation. He names them as his people. In Psalm 67 we meet the blessing of Aaron again. The psalm quotes the blessing and then tells us the reason why God names his people and blesses them:

> May God be gracious to us and bless us
>   and make his face shine on us –
> so that your ways may be known on earth,
>   your salvation among all nations.
> (verses 1–2)

The covenant shapes God's people for mission. It shows what it means to be a witnessing people. The book of Ruth is a lovely cameo of this in action. When God's people live under God's law (like the law of gleaning), vulnerable, immigrant widows find blessing, peace and hope among the community of God's people. As Boaz says to Ruth, 'May you be richly rewarded by the LORD, the God of Israel, under whose wings you have come to take refuge' (Ruth 2:12). Israel was not only to make God known to the nations; they were also to welcome people from other nations: 'You are to love those who are foreigners, for you yourselves were foreigners in Egypt' (Deuteronomy 10:19).

The threat of the nations

The nations are objects of God's grace expressed through the witness of his people. But the nations and their gods are also a threat to the people of God. Throughout history, the people of God – first Israel and then the church – are in conflict with the world around them. The world divides into two humanities or two cities. Humanity in opposition to God persecutes the people of God. It's Egypt, then Canaan, then Philistia, then Assyria, then Babylon, then Rome. Sometimes it's presented in mythical terms, as in Ezekiel's vision of Gog and

Magog (Ezekiel 38 – 39). The most common expression of this conflict is the contrast between Babylon and Jerusalem, which the apostle John picks up in the book of Revelation. Babel becomes Babylon – the symbol of humanity in opposition to God and his people.

When Joshua takes the land of Canaan, he's told to destroy everyone and everything belonging to the Canaanite nations. Everything is said to be 'devoted to destruction' (Joshua 6:21 ESV). This is an act of judgment against those nations. God delayed giving the land to Abraham's family because 'the sin of the Amorites has not yet reached its full measure' (Genesis 15:16). It prefigures the final day of judgment. But this destruction is also intended to protect God's people from the influence of the nations. God's people will either be a light to the nations or they'll be corrupted by the nations.

The rise and fall of Israel's witness

In the reign of Solomon, Israel reaches its zenith as a light to the nations, but the seeds of its failure are sown also. The Queen of Sheba travels from the ends of the world to hear God's wisdom from Solomon (1 Kings 4:34; 10:1–13). The nations bring their wealth to enrich God's people and God's temple (1 Kings 10:14–29). But Solomon also marries foreign wives who bring with them their foreign gods (1 Kings 11:1–3). Solomon himself joins in their worship (1 Kings 11:4–8). The call to be a light to the nations and the threat from the nations are both there in his reign. 'The tragedy of Solomon's reign,' says Philip Hacking, 'was that instead of influencing the world for God, the Jewish nation had been influenced by the world away from godly standards.'[3]

The writer of Kings assesses the kings of Israel in accordance with the calling to be a light to the nations. The Lord drove out the wicked nations of Canaan so that there might be a place on earth where the goodness of his rule could be seen by the nations. The tragedy of Israel is that it reverted to the ways of those wicked nations: 'The people engaged in all the detestable practices of the nations the LORD had driven out before the Israelites' (1 Kings 14:24; see also 2 Kings 16:3; 17:8, 11, 15, 33; 21:2). The nation reaches the point of no return under the reign of Manasseh: 'Manasseh led them astray, so that they did more evil than the nations the LORD had destroyed before the Israelites' (2 Kings 21:9). They are no longer a light to the nations. They don't even follow the ways of the nations. They're actually *more* evil than the nations now.

The God of all nations

As a result, God uses the nations to judge Israel. Ezekiel 4 – 24 contains Ezekiel's warning of judgment to God's people. He uses two repeated refrains: 'Then they will know that I am the LORD' and 'I am against you'. In chapters 25 – 32 Ezekiel addresses the surrounding nations one by one. The same two refrains are repeated throughout these chapters. The message to the nations is the *same message* as that to Israel:

- The nations should not misunderstand Israel's downfall: Israel's God is their God. They should not suppose that their triumph over Israel means their gods are more powerful: 'You will know that I am the LORD.' The Lord is the God of all the earth. Ezekiel begins with a vision of a moving throne to show that God is not limited to one location (Ezekiel 1:1, 3, 15–28).
- The nations should not delight in Israel's downfall: Israel's fate will be their fate. The nations are also told:

'I am against you' (26:3; 28:22; 29:3, 10; 30:22). The exile of Israel is a picture of humanity's fate – we will all be defeated by God and eternally exiled from the blessing of his reign.

This is Ezekiel's theology of mission. Israel should have been a blessing to the nations. Instead, they profaned God's holy name before the nations. But where Israel fails, God himself will act:

> Therefore say to the Israelites, 'This is what the Sovereign LORD says: it is not for your sake, people of Israel, that I am going to do these things, but for the sake of my holy name, which you have profaned among the nations where you have gone. I will show the holiness of my great name, which has been profaned among the nations, the name you have profaned among them. Then the nations will know that I am the LORD, declares the Sovereign LORD, when I am proved holy through you before their eyes.'
> (Ezekiel 36:22–23)

A renewed missionary identity

The prophets tell us that the new thing God is going to do for Israel will encompass the nations (Isaiah 11:10–16; 19:18–25). 'Right through the prophetic ministry,' says Philip Hacking, 'there is still the vision of the world which would turn to the God of Israel.'[4] 'Many nations,' says God, 'will become my people' (Zechariah 2:11). God will gather his people scattered in exile, but at the same time he will gather people from the four corners of the world (Isaiah 56:6–8; 66:18–21). The song of God's praise will go into all the earth (Isaiah 12:5–6). The apostle James quotes from

Amos 9:11–12 at the Council of Jerusalem to argue that
Gentiles can be part of the church:

> . . . I will return
>   and rebuild David's fallen tent . . .
> that the rest of mankind may seek the Lord,
>   even all the Gentiles [or nations] who bear my name.
> (Acts 15:16–17)

Israel had failed to model life under the rule of God in a way
that attracted the nations. But the prophets promise that one
day the nations will be drawn to God (Isaiah 2:1–5; Micah
4:1–5). Isaiah promised that the 'servant of the LORD' is
coming. The servant will succeed where Israel failed:

- I will keep you and will make you
      to be a covenant for the people
      and a light for the Gentiles [= nations].
  (Isaiah 42:6)

- I will also make you a light for the Gentiles [= nations],
      that my salvation may reach to the ends of the earth.
  (Isaiah 49:6)

In Jonah we have the story of a Gentile nation that repents in
response to the preaching of God's word. Jonah runs from
God's commission to go to Nineveh not because he's afraid,
but because he knows God is gracious (2 Kings 14:23–27). He
suspects God will save Nineveh and he doesn't want grace to
extend to Israel's enemies (Jonah 4:2). But in the waters of the
ocean Jonah experiences something of the godforsakenness
of the nations and in that experience rediscovers the grace
of God:

From deep in the realm of the dead I called for help,
    and you listened to my cry . . .
Those who cling to worthless idols
    turn away from God's love for them.
But I, with shouts of grateful praise,
    will sacrifice to you.
What I have vowed I will make good.
    I will say, 'Salvation comes from the LORD.'
(Jonah 2:2, 8–9)

Jonah learns a new compassion for the nations that takes him to Nineveh (even if his compassion proves to be short-lived).

Jonah's autobiography is a prophetic call to Israel to have compassion on the nations. Its message is the same for us today. Our experience of God's grace compels us to demonstrate that grace and declare it to the nations.

5

The hope of the nations

The prophet Isaiah promised that God would send a servant to be a light to the nations. With that promise still ringing in our ears, we hear Jesus say, 'I am the light of the world' (John 8:12). (See also John 1:4–9; 3:19–21; 9:5; 12:46; Acts 13:47.)

Imagine getting lost at night in the woods. In the darkness you can't find the path. Instead, you stumble through the undergrowth, suspecting that you're going around in circles. And then someone appears with a bright torch. They can show you the way home. This is what Israel was supposed to do for the nations. The nations were stumbling around in the dark, unable to find their way back to God. But God called Israel to model life under his good rule. They were to display his character. They were to be holy, as he is holy. Their life together was to be the proof that God is good to know (Deuteronomy 4:5–8). Yet instead, Israel profaned his name (Romans 2:19, 24).

God, however, has not left us in the dark. When Jesus came into the world, 'the true light that gives light to everyone was coming into the world' (John 1:9). Jesus is the fulfilment of Israel's calling to be a missionary people who make God known to the nations. Jesus perfectly represents God to the world. He brings the light of salvation to humanity in darkness. He *is* that light. Jesus is the one 'in [whose] name the nations will put their hope' (Matthew 12:15–21).

The Jews expected that one day God would gather the scattered people of Israel. It is Jesus who does this. But he will also gather people from the four corners of the world (Mark 13:27). The nation of Israel has the priority in his earthly ministry (Matthew 10:5–6; 15:21–28), but as the nation and its leaders reject him, so the gospel goes to all those who will receive the good news, both Jews or Gentiles.

Luke begins his account of Jesus' ministry with a sermon at Nazareth which defines his ministry. Jesus reads from Isaiah 61:1–2 and claims that this is fulfilled in himself. So far, so good. 'All spoke well of him and were amazed at the gracious words that came from his lips' (Luke 4:22). But then Jesus predicts (or perhaps precipitates) their rejection of him by highlighting the way that Elijah fed only a Gentile widow and Elisha healed only a Gentile soldier (4:24–27). The people welcome the news of the promised salvation, but they're 'furious' at the suggestion that salvation might come to other nations ahead of the Jews (4:28–30). Then in Luke 7 Jesus heals the servant of a Gentile soldier and raises the son of a Gentile widow (as Elijah did), enacting what he's spoken about in 4:24–27. The salvation that Jesus brings will include people from all nations: 'People will come from east and west and north and south, and will take their places at the feast in the kingdom of God' (Luke 13:29).

A King for the nations

Why do we go and make disciples of all nations? The answer of Matthew 28 is because all authority has been given to the risen Christ:

> Then Jesus came to them and said, 'All authority in heaven
> and on earth has been given to me. Therefore go and make
> disciples of all nations, baptising them in the name of the
> Father and of the Son and of the Holy Spirit, and teaching
> them to obey everything I have commanded you. And surely
> I am with you always, to the very end of the age.'
> (Matthew 28:18–20)

In raising Jesus from the dead, 'God has made this Jesus,
whom you crucified, both Lord and Messiah' (Acts 2:36). His
resurrection is his enthronement. The trial on earth which
declared him to be a blasphemer and traitor has been over-
turned by the heavenly court of appeal. Jesus is about to
ascend, as promised in Daniel 7, to receive from the Ancient
of Days 'an everlasting dominion that will not pass away, and
his kingdom is one that will never be destroyed'. 'He was
given authority, glory and sovereign power,' promises Daniel.
'All nations and peoples of every language worshipped him'
(Daniel 7:14).

Because Jesus has been given authority over the nations, he
sends his disciples out to call the nations to submit to that
authority. He exercises his rule on earth through the proclamation of his word. We are ambassadors of Christ, bringing an
announcement from the King. Whenever we proclaim the
gospel, we're heralds of the coming King. It's as if we go to
the citizens of a country and say that a king is coming who
rightly claims their allegiance. Those who currently rule them
are usurpers and tyrants. But the true King is coming and he
will reign (Mark 12:1–11).

This is what takes place in evangelism. We declare that Jesus
is King and that Jesus *will be* King. The earliest encapsulation
of the Christian message was: 'Jesus is Lord' – confessed at a
time when the rest of the world was declaring Caesar to be

Lord (Romans 10:9). Jesus has been given all authority by the Father, and one day every knee will bow before him. If people acknowledge his lordship now, they'll experience his coming rule as blessing, life and salvation. If they reject him, they'll experience his coming rule as conquest, death and judgment.

Much of our evangelism takes an individual you-and-God approach: you have sinned, your sin cuts you off from God, but Jesus removes the consequences of sin so you can know God again. There is nothing incorrect about this story. But the Bible tells a much bigger, fuller story. It is the story of God creating a new humanity, reasserting his life-giving, liberating rule over the world, and bringing it to a climax in the triumph of his Son and the renewal of creation. The danger of the you-and-God message is that I remain at the centre. I am the almighty consumer, shopping around for what suits me best, with God providing the best option for my religious life. God serves my spiritual needs, while Tesco serves my grocery needs. And the customer is always right. The Bible story, by contrast, puts God firmly at the centre. The gospel tells the story of the kingdom of God. The goal of the story is the glory of God, and the climax of the story is: 'God . . . all in all' (1 Corinthians 15:28).

That declaration is anticipated in the cross and resurrection. The resurrection is the promise that the godlessness and god-forsakenness of the cross is not the last word. God's kingdom is coming. Eternal life is coming. A new creation is coming.

A community for the nations

It is not just Jesus who is described as the light of the world. In the Sermon on the Mount Jesus says,

> You are the light of the world. A town built on a hill cannot be hidden. Neither do people light a lamp and put it under a

bowl. Instead they put it on its stand, and it gives light to everyone in the house. In the same way, let your light shine before others, that they may see your good deeds and glorify your Father in heaven.

(Matthew 5:14–16)

Jesus is talking to his disciples (Matthew 5:1). The new community of Jesus is the light of the world and a city built on a hill. We need to read these verses with the Old Testament in mind.

As we saw in the previous chapter, Israel was called to be a light to the nations, to live under God's law so that the nations would be attracted to Israel's God. But the opposite happened. Instead of attracting the nations to the ways of God, Israel was attracted to the ways of the nations. But now Jesus' disciples will be a light to the world.

Jerusalem was the city on a hill to which the nations would come and from which God's word would go forth to the nations (Isaiah 2:1–5). 'Great is the LORD,' sang the psalmist, 'and most worthy of praise, in the city of our God, his holy mountain. Beautiful in its loftiness, the joy of the whole earth' (Psalm 48:1–2). God's intention was for the whole earth to find joy in Jerusalem because God was there, living with his people. But again, it didn't work out like that. Jerusalem was not faithful to God. So the nations come to Jerusalem not to worship God, but to plunder and destroy. But now Jesus' new community will be the city on a hill that draws people to God.

The Christian community is both a sign and a promise of God's coming liberation. That is how we communicate the good news of Jesus. People who won't listen to eloquent and sophisticated arguments will be persuaded by authentic lives, by genuine community, by loving relationships, by flawed people who know the grace of God.

But here's the challenge: 'Neither do people light a lamp and put it under a bowl. Instead they put it on its stand, and it gives light to everyone in the house' (Matthew 5:15). Our light must be seen. We need to be out there in the world, introducing our unbelieving friends to our Christian friends. Having a great community is not enough. We need to reach out beyond the community, welcoming others and pointing them to the Father.

It's sometimes said that mission in the Old Testament was centripetal (in towards the centre), but that mission in the New Testament is now centrifugal (out from the centre). There's clearly some truth in this. We're to go out to the nations. But we're also to attract the nations, just as Israel was to do in the Old Testament. What's changed is the centre! The nations no longer stream into Jerusalem, to Israel, to Zion. They're drawn to the new Jerusalem, the new Israel, the church.

The Bible story ends with a vision of a restored Eden with a tree of life fed by the water that flows from the throne of the Lamb. 'The leaves of the tree,' we discover, 'are for the healing of the nations' (Revelation 22:2). All the nations will come to worship God (Revelation 15:3–4):

After this I looked, and there before me was a great multitude that no one could count, from every nation, tribe, people and language, standing before the throne and before the Lamb. They were wearing white robes and were holding palm branches in their hands. And they cried out in a loud voice:

'Salvation belongs to our God,
who sits on the throne,
and to the Lamb.'
(Revelation 7:9–10)

Not only are representatives from every nation in the new creation, but they bring the best of their culture to enrich it: 'The nations will walk by its light, and the kings of the earth will bring their splendour into it . . . The glory and honour of the nations will be brought into it' (Revelation 21:24, 26).

'All peoples on earth will be blessed through you,' said God to Abraham (Genesis 12:3). This was the vision that propelled Paul to proclaim the gospel throughout the known world. And today the promise of blessing to the nations, first given to Abraham, anticipated in the life of the church and fulfilled around the throne of the Lamb, is still the vision that propels us to the ends of the earth.

The story is not yet over

In this and the previous chapter we have traced the story of mission through the Old and New Testaments. That story is not yet over. The Bible itself, of course, is now complete. But the church continues to grow, and its mission continues to bear fruit. The book of Acts is peppered with summary statements about the spread of God's word: 'The word of God continued to spread and flourish'; 'The word of the Lord spread widely and grew in power' (Acts 12:24; 19:20; see also 2:41–47; 6:7; 9:31; 16:5). Paul tells the Colossian church, 'The gospel is bearing fruit and growing throughout the whole world – just as it has been doing among you since the day you heard it and truly understood God's grace' (1:6).

Today God's word continues 'to spread and flourish'. 'I am not ashamed of the gospel,' says Paul in Romans 1:16, 'because it is the power of God that brings salvation to everyone who believes.' Today the gospel is still the power of God and is still bringing people to salvation.

A week after I finished the first draft of this book, I was speaking at a Bible convention in Argyll. At our first meal I found myself sitting next to Jangkholam 'Lamboi' Haokip, a church leader from Manipur in north-east India. I happened to mention that I had been writing a book on world mission for Keswick Ministries. Immediately, Lamboi said, 'Watkin Roberts, the man who brought the gospel to my people, committed himself to mission at the Keswick Convention in 1907.' He told me his story, and what a story it is.[1]

Roberts was a quarryman in a Welsh slate mine. The Welsh revival in 1904 had had a big impact on him, and reaching those who had never heard of Christ became the driving passion of his life. He had no formal qualifications, but devoted his spare time to reading the Bible and theology books. He first dedicated himself to go as a missionary at the Keswick Convention in 1907. At the Convention Roberts met Dr Peter Fraser who told him about the needs in north-east India and invited him to join him in establishing a clinic in Aizawl. Roberts was still only twenty-two when they arrived there in December 1908, and the local people nicknamed him 'Mr Youngman'.

'Because he lacked formal education and refused to support denomination-based mission,' explained Lamboi, 'he wasn't recognized by a mission agency, but he lit a fire in the region!' Roberts wanted to reach the Kuki territory, but the British authorities refused him permission to enter the area. At that time the Kuki people were notorious headhunters and one of the most feared tribes in India.

In 1909 Roberts received a gift of £5 from a Miss Emily Davies. He used the money to buy newly translated copies of John's Gospel in the related Lushai language, which he then sent as gifts to village chiefs in the area. Several months later a letter arrived from Chief Kamkholun Singson, chief of the largest village in the area. 'Sir, come yourself, and tell us about this book and your God,' he wrote.

Even with this letter of invitation, the local British agent refused Roberts permission. 'When I go there,' he explained, 'I take along a hundred soldiers for protection, and I can't spare a single soldier for you.' Roberts ignored this warning and went anyway, armed only with the word of God.

After a week of teaching, five men became Christians, including the Chief. Roberts went back to Aizawl and appointed local leaders to continue the work. Those early preachers founded churches in almost every village.

Roberts himself was branded a troublemaker by the British authorities and he was eventually deported before he could complete the translation of the Bible. So the Kuki people appointed one of their own, Rochunga Pudaite, to be trained to complete the work.

Speaking of his people today, Pudaite says, 'At least ninety-five percent are Christians, worshipping in over 200 churches. Except for Mr Roberts, the only missionary they have had is the Bible.'[2] They have levels of literacy, school enrolment and healthcare far above national averages in India, and many have gone on to make significant contributions at a national level. They are also taking responsibility for the task of world mission, sending more than 16 million copies of the New Testament to homes around the world.

That is not a bad return on an investment of £5!

Part three:
The scope of mission

6

Who? Everyone with the church at its heart

John was a horticultural lecturer. But God had placed in his heart a desire to serve Christ in India. In 1970 he had attended the Keswick Convention as part of a group that included a young woman called Alison. 'I still have my notes on Alec Motyer's five Bible readings on Amos: "Chosen, Called and Faithful". I'm sure that during those readings (crammed together on uncomfortable wooden benches) the Spirit was planting his seeds in the receptive soil of our souls as we struggled with whether the Lord wanted us to serve together.'[1] By the end of the Convention they were engaged, and together they went forward at the World Mission Evening as a sign of their commitment to go as a couple. Over the years people like John from all walks of life have walked to the front for prayer and advice at one of the evening celebrations as a sign of their commitment to serve Christ overseas.

Anyone can go

The first missionaries in the Christian church included several fishermen, a tax collector and a political zealot. Today we might say they included manual labourers, entrepreneurs, professionals and political activists. In Acts 4 Peter and John proclaim Christ before the religious leaders. We're told, 'When they saw the courage of Peter and John and realised that they were unschooled, ordinary men, they were astonished and they took note that these men had been with Jesus' (Acts 4:13).

They were uneducated. You don't need a degree to be a missionary. It may help to get some training, but don't think mission is only for people who've been to university.

They were ordinary. You don't need to be some kind of super-Christian. You should already be serving God in your current situation. But you don't need to enjoy an hour-long quiet time every day, have perfect children and be leading five young people to Christ every week. Mission is for ordinary people.

Here's what you do need though – you need to know Jesus: 'They took note that these men had been with Jesus.' You need to have a passion for Jesus.

The great apostle Paul wrote to the Corinthians, 'I came to you in weakness with great fear, and trembling' (1 Corinthians 2:3). Perhaps that's how you feel about the thought of going as a missionary: weakness, fear, trembling. He goes on to say, 'My message and my preaching were not with wise and persuasive words.' Maybe you've not got a degree. Maybe you can't imagine persuading someone to be a Christian. Maybe you don't know all the answers to the questions people might ask. Maybe you're not good at public speaking. It doesn't matter, because Paul goes on, 'My message and my preaching were not with wise and persuasive words, but with a demonstration of the Spirit's power, so that your faith might not rest on human wisdom, but on God's power' (1 Corinthians 2:4–5).

It's important to realize how radical Paul is. He's not simply saying that it doesn't matter if you're weak or ordinary. He's saying it's a positive advantage. It creates space for God's power. Imagine a very eloquent or persuasive or dynamic person, the sort of individual who readily attracts a following. Such a person would be the ideal missionary, we might suppose. But Paul disagrees. They might well win a following, but when someone just as dynamic comes along, people will follow them instead. Or when flaws in their character appear, people will be devastated because their faith was tied up with that individual.

The messenger matches the message. And this is our message: 'we preach Christ crucified: a stumbling-block to Jews and foolishness to Gentiles' (1 Corinthians 1:23). It's important to follow Paul's logic. He says, 'When I came to you, I did not come with eloquence or human wisdom as I proclaimed to you the testimony about God. For I resolved to know nothing while I was with you except Jesus Christ and him crucified' (1 Corinthians 2:1–2). Notice the word 'for'. Why did Paul avoid eloquence and human wisdom? 'For' he preached Christ crucified. We can't preach in a triumphalist, strident or arrogant manner a Saviour who saves by dying in weakness and shame.

Instead, we make room for God's power in weakness. 'For the message of the cross is foolishness to those who are perishing, but to us who are being saved it is the power of God' (1 Corinthians 1:18). The world may view the cross as weakness and folly, 'but to those whom God has called, both Jews and Greeks, Christ the power of God and the wisdom of God' (1 Corinthians 1:24). We might be weak, but our words come with 'a demonstration of the Spirit's power'. As a result, people's faith does 'not rest on human wisdom, but on God's power' (1 Corinthians 2:4–5). As Paul puts in his second letter to the Corinthians, 'We have this treasure in jars of clay to show that this all-surpassing power is from God and not from us' (2 Corinthians 4:7).

Feeling weak, ill-equipped and uneducated are not impediments to getting involved in mission. Rather, they're among the qualifications required! What matters is that you have a passion for Jesus. In 1987 George Verwer told the Keswick Convention,

> When I came to Britain in 1962 with the vision for Operation Mobilisation, people just laughed – it was a joke. But three months later, ninety British young people crossed the channel. Twelve months later, two thousand (nine hundred of them British) went, and they have never stopped. As you go, as you obey, others will follow.[2]

You will have gathered by now that there are a hundred jobs to do in mission. It's not all about preaching sermons or being missionary doctors. There are people involved in logistics, administration, IT support, marketing and childcare. If you're employed where you are now, there's every chance that those skills are needed somewhere in the context of world mission. There are also many people whose role is to make friends and tell people about the Best Friend. If you have friends where you are now, then you could be someone who makes friends in a country where few people have heard of Jesus.

Age is also no barrier, as John's story will go on to illustrate. Having returned from eight years' service in India, John and Alison settled down to raise a family in the UK. And that might have been that. Except that, aged fifty, they felt called again to mission and again went forward at a Keswick missionary evening, this time together with their seventeen-year-old daughter. They went to the Indian subcontinent on a business visa and set up a project providing sets of books to pastors at low cost. During their first year, however, Alison was diagnosed with cancer, so eventually she supported the project from the UK while John 'commuted' to India. Altogether, 18,000 book sets, each containing forty-five books, were distributed at thirty-six three-day conferences training pastors how to use them. Finally, John handed over the project so that he could care full-time for Alison. In 2000, the last year of Alison's life, they attended the Convention with the help of the missionary support fund. They heard John Stott speak on power through weakness from 1 Corinthians. 'This,' writes John, 'is something Alison lived with and witnessed to as her journey neared its heavenly destination.'[3]

Again, that might have been the end of the story. But in 2012 John attended a seminar track at the Convention on 'the third age' and was challenged to think what God might want him to do with his 'extra time'. It was a call confirmed by Psalm 92:14: 'They will still bear fruit in old age, they will stay fresh and green.' When I met him, he was about to return to overseas service for a third time, now aged seventy, to provide pastoral and administrative support to others pursuing their calling.

Another great opportunity in mission is 'tentmaking'. Tentmakers are people who don't raise support or get paid by a mission agency. Instead, they get a job locally or run a business so that they are self-supported. They're called 'tent-makers' after the apostle Paul, who often supported himself by making tents (Acts 18:2–4). Sometimes people opt to become tentmakers because this is the only way in which to gain access to a country otherwise closed to missionaries. Sometimes they do so because it's a great way to build relationships with people or contribute to a country's economic development. Sometimes individuals are assigned by their company to work overseas and choose to view this as an opportunity to serve the local church.

David and Ruth Burgos have served in Spain for over fifteen years. They're involved in church leadership and evangelism as well as having a prayer ministry and a children's ministry – almost completely supported by their business. 'God has given us a prospering business in Barcelona,' David told me at the 2013 Keswick Convention. 'I started it in 2001, and it's given me and my wife many engaging experiences explaining Christ to people who would never enter a church.'

Anyone with a passion for Jesus can be sent to serve in world mission. But local churches should have a commitment to *sending their best people*. Over the years I have met some oddballs in mission. It quickly became apparent that they were the misfits who wanted to serve, but never really cut it at home. So it was convenient to ship them off elsewhere. Mission isn't a way of getting rid of your misfits. Send your best instead.

Mission is not a zero-sum game where your loss is someone else's gain. The economy of God doesn't work like that. If you send your best, God is no-one's debtor. He will replenish what you think you're losing. Other people might step up to fill the gaps left by the people you've sent. Plus, sending people in world mission provokes mission at home.

We really need a different view of success. Even at a purely numerical level we need better indicators than the number in your congregation or the size of your budget. A better numerical measure would be the people you have sent and the churches you have planted. Imagine a church that evangelizes people in its local area, disciples them and then sends so many of them on to needy areas that it never grows numerically. Now that would be a great ambition for a local church!

Everyone is involved

Not everyone will go. Indeed, not everyone can go. But still, every Christian has the joy and responsibility of being involved in world mission. We can all serve as senders. In 1987 Gavin Reid told the Keswick Convention how he was once taken to visit an elderly lady in a little house in Toxteth, Liverpool. He goes on,

> My companion asked, 'Well now, Molly, where are you today?' I thought it was a very odd question! But she replied immediately, 'South America.' I looked around her little living room and there on her table was all the prayer material for the South American Missionary Society. It was Tuesday morning, and she was in South America. That afternoon she would be in India or somewhere else. Wednesday she spent in England. She rarely took her body out of that little house, but her prayers circled the world.[4]

Here are some ideas for supporting mission and missionaries as a local church:

Creating a passion for mission

- Develop a plan for your church's involvement in world mission that includes how you're going to decide who to support, what your priorities will be and ways to ensure it has a high profile within your church.
- Consider developing a focus or foci as a church so that you can develop specialist understanding, concentrate your efforts and create a sense of ownership. Instead of having a little involvement in many areas, think about doing one or two things really well.

- Suggest that each home group, children's group or family 'adopt' a missionary or a mission prayer focus.
- Organize a short-term team. Ensure that short-term teams understand they're going primarily to learn and be inspired rather than save the world!
- Include stories from your missionaries in your sermons.

Keeping informed about mission

- Ensure that everyone in your church is kept up to date and remembers your missionaries. Use your bulletin, a notice board, slots in the Sunday meetings, prayer meetings and circulate prayer letters.
- Ensure that new people who join your church know about your missionaries. Include this in courses for new members.
- Subscribe to some of the magazines and prayer bulletins of mission agencies.
- Attend mission conferences.
- Include a country focus in your prayer meetings.
- Use *Operation World*, which provides information for prayer on every country in the world.[5] This resource is divided so you can pray for different countries every day throughout the year. Or use *Operation World* to provide a mission perspective when you pray for current news stories.

Supporting missionaries in the field

- Treat your missionaries as other church staff members so that you budget to pay them a proper wage and

provide proper appraisals. Don't do gimmicky
fundraisers for them unless you also do gimmicky
fundraisers for your pastor! Instead, teach the
congregation the importance of regular and sustained
support for world mission. Commit as a church to
underwrite your missionaries' financial support so they
don't need to worry about fundraising while they're
out on the field.

- Pray for their relationship with God, their physical and
emotional needs, family relationships, language
learning, effective ministry, team relationships and
country of service.[6]
- Send people to visit your missionaries – including your
pastor.
- Send letters or emails to your missionaries with news
from your church, your family and the wider culture.
Send them a copy of your church magazine or bulletin
so that they know what's happening at home.
- Be conscientious about following any guidelines on
what can be said publicly about the ministry of your
missionaries if they're in a country that doesn't
welcome missionaries.
- Remember their birthdays with a phone call, a text,
an email or a card.
- Give your missionaries a Kindle or iPad so you can
readily send them eBooks and Christian music over
the internet. If you have a recommended 'book of the
term', for example, then send it to them. Give your
missionaries a subscription to a Christian magazine
or a magazine connected with their hobby.
- Send parcels with 'goodies' from home – personal
messages along with things your missionaries can't
readily buy where they are.

- Stick their photo on your fridge or keep it in your Bible so that you're prompted to pray for them regularly.
- Phone or Skype your missionary during your home group or prayer meeting.

Supporting missionaries on furlough (home leave) or when they return

- Let people know what missionaries will need when they return and ensure that they have all their immediate practical needs met (a home, a car, food in the cupboards, the first few meals, and so on).
- Have a debrief with your missionaries and identify any changes that need to take place. Make sure you include in this a discussion of their financial needs.
- Give your missionaries a guide to cultural and technological changes.
- Give your missionaries opportunities to tell people about their work. Invite them to speak on a Sunday morning to signal this is 'mainstream' and important to your church.
- Invite missionaries to speak to children's and young people's groups.
- Try not to overload them with travel and deputation so that they have time to rest and reconnect with their sending church.
- Give your missionaries opportunities to contribute to 'ordinary' church life.
- Send your missionaries to a conference or retreat that will refresh or stimulate them.
- Invite missionaries to meals and outings or offer to babysit.
- Invite your missionaries to give their reflections on church life and mission at home.

The importance of the local church

Paul consistently puts the local church at the heart of mission. Think for a moment about his approach.

1. Paul is sent by a local church

Paul is sent by a local church and reports back to a local church (Acts 13:1–3; 14:27–28). He is not sent by a mission agency, nor does he report to anyone other than his local church. Of course not, because there were no mission agencies at the time! Mission agencies only came into being because local churches stopped doing their job of sending people. Today they have a role as specialist advisers, but mission belongs to the local church.

2. Paul goes with a team to model church

Paul always takes team members: Barnabas, Silas, Timothy, Titus, Luke. He wants support and he wants co-workers. And he wants a team that will demonstrate Christian community so that unbelievers can see the gospel in action and new believers have a model of church to follow. The team functions as a church even as a church grows up around it, providing a context for discipleship and a demonstration of Christian community.

3. Paul's aim is to plant churches

Everywhere he goes, Paul wants to leave behind a church. Yes, he proclaimed the gospel. Yes, he helped the poor. But his goal was to start a church, so that the church could continue to proclaim the gospel and help the poor after he had left.

4. Paul establishes churches by leaving

Paul moves on. In doing so, he creates space for churches to develop without him so that new leaders can emerge and the new churches don't become dependent on him.

5. Paul creates mission partnerships between churches

Paul refuses to let one church come under the authority of another (Galatians 1:11–24; 2:6–9). He doesn't want a church to be *dependent* on other churches. But at the same time, he pursues relationships between churches (2:1–3). He doesn't want churches to be *independent*. He wants partnership in mission.

Mission belongs to the local church.

The importance of church planting

What's striking about Paul's approach is that the church was at the heart of both ends of his mission, both sending people from home and mission in the field. The church was not only central to how people were sent; it was also central to what they did when they arrived.

For Paul, mission meant planting churches. In the New Testament, wherever the gospel was preached, local churches were established. Paul planted churches that would continue his mission by being missionary churches. Planting was built into their nature. Paul planted churches as a bridge into a city. They would reach that city by continually adding further household congregations. A vision for church growth must be a vision for church planting.

1. Church planting puts mission at the heart of the Christian community

It's all too easy for churches to institutionalize or even fossilize over time. Mission becomes one activity among others. Or it's left to the enthusiasts to get on with it at the fringes. Church planting, however, inevitably and naturally shifts the church back into missionary mode. Suddenly, mission once again defines the nature, purpose and activity of the church – both for the new church plant and for the sending church. In the sending church, people have to step up to roles that others have left unfilled, and the gaps confront the congregation afresh with the challenge of mission.

2. Church planting puts the Christian community at the heart of mission

God's purposes are not focused on many unrelated individuals, but upon his people. Christ died for the elect, for his bride, for the church. The Bible is the story of God creating a new humanity, a new people who will be his people. If individuals were at the heart of God's purposes, then it would be quite natural to put the individual at the heart of mission – and many people do that. But at the heart of God's plan of salvation are a family and a nation. And so the church should be at the heart of mission.

To be a Christian is, by definition, to be part of the community of God's people. To be united with Christ is to be part of his body. The assumption of the New Testament is that this always finds expression in commitment to a local church. The centrality of the church means the centrality of the congregation or it means nothing. Some people take a fluid view of church in the name of the universal church. They go to a conference, join a short-term team, participate in a parachurch organization, claiming that all these constitute their commitment to the church. There may be some validity in calling these things church in some sense. But they are not a substitute for the community that the New Testament presupposes is the context of the Christian life. It is easy to love the church in the abstract or to love people short term. But we are called to love people as we share our lives with them. This is the pathway to Christian growth and holiness. Commitment to the people of God is expressed through commitment to specific congregations.

So mission cannot be done by a lone ranger. It must be done by a community of believers. It cannot be done in hit-and-run raids. There must be a community that can be observed and that offers a place of belonging. When we think 'mission', we must think 'church'. And the best way to link church and mission is through church planting.

Some missionaries see church planting as their primary commitment. They regard development work as a diversion from this primary task or as merely a means to get into a country closed to missionaries. Sometimes this can mean that their commitment to good development work is notional. Other groups want to be very professional about their development work. But they have little commitment to church planting, and the project is everything. In one country that I visited a few years ago, few foreign workers had bothered to learn the language. They did projects using a translator. This looks good in the marketing, but it's not creating sustainable Christian mission. Sustainable Christian evangelism or discipleship or development or social action all require sustainable Christian communities. Without a local church, whatever you do will end when you go. And only if you leave behind a local church will the work of mission continue.

Arvid was the pastor of a young church in eastern Europe. Now he's leading a small church planting team in an unreached country. It's a city of 70,000 people, and the team are the only Christians in the city. Sending their pastor was a massive decision for that small church. For three years they sent small teams to the city three times a year so that everyone caught the vision. Then a team of eight stayed for three months, researching the culture and make-up of the city. Arvid described how making the decision involved lots of coffee and talking to people so that they felt part of what was happening.

This church planting team in this unreached city is the result of one small church taking responsibility for mission.

Arvid and his team are planting with Damien and Sarah, a married couple from a church in the UK. The husband used to be a postal worker. Their church was praying for people to work with Arvid, and their leader asked if anyone felt God suggesting a name. Sarah said, 'Yes . . . mine.' When she told Damien, he hit the roof. But now there they are with their three young children working under Arvid's leadership. This church planting team in this unreached city is a partnership of local churches.

Who does mission? Everyone. Damien and Sarah were not preachers, pastors or doctors. They were 'ordinary' Christians who went to do ordinary Christianity in an unreached part of the world.

Whose responsibility is mission? The local church. Arvid, Damien and Sarah were sent by their churches. Their churches were helped by a mission agency (in this case, Radstock Ministries). But it was the local churches that took responsibility for sending them. And the local church was not only central in sending them; it was central to their aims. Their aim was to evangelize the lost, disciple converts and form them into a new church.

7

What? Everything with proclamation at the centre

Ruth and Vishal Mangalwadi begin their appreciation of William Carey with a fictional quiz.[1] Carey was one of the first Western missionaries to India, arriving in 1793. The Mangalwadis imagine a competition for Indian university students in which the question asked is: 'Who was William Carey?'

The first reply is that William Carey was a botanist who published the first books on the natural history of India, who introduced new systems of gardening, and after whom a variety of eucalyptus is named. Next, an engineering student says that William Carey introduced the steam engine to India and began the first indigenous paper and printing industries. Another student sees Carey as a social reformer who success-fully campaigned for women's rights. Another says that he was a campaigner for the humane treatment of leprosy sufferers. An economics student points out that Carey intro-duced savings banks to combat usury. Carey is credited with starting the first newspaper in any oriental language. He conducted a systematic survey of Indian agricultural practices and founded the Indian Agri-Horticultural Society, thirty years before the Royal Agricultural Society was established in England. Carey was the first to translate and publish the classic religious texts of India, and he wrote the first Sanskrit dictionary for scholars. He founded dozen of schools, providing education for people of all castes, both boys and girls. He pioneered lending libraries and wrote the first essays on forestry in India. To a significant degree, he transformed the ethos of the British administration in India from colonial exploitation to a genuine sense of civil service.

And so it goes on, with Carey's contribution to science, engineering, industry, economics, medicine, agriculture and forestry, literature, education, social reform, public adminis-tration and philosophy all being celebrated. Yet most of us know William Carey as the cobbler from Northamptonshire who became a pioneer missionary and evangelist. Who was the real William Carey? The answer is that Carey was all of these things and more.

The word 'mission', as we've already noted, means 'sending'. Mission begins with God sending his Son into the world to redeem the world. Jesus says, 'As the Father has sent me, I am sending you' (John 20:21). Mission involves all that Jesus sends us into the world to do. So people from Keswick have gone around the world to do a huge variety of things: as evangelists, church planters, lecturers, Bible translators, pastors, but also as doctors, teachers, journalists, engineers, advocates, peace-makers, administrators, lawyers, pilots and community facilitators. People have gone to plant churches, campaign for justice, dig wells, transform slums, shelter street children, care for the environment, rehabilitate addicts, build schools – showing love and bringing change in the name of Jesus.

Each year at the Keswick Convention the Earthworks exhibition features the work of mission agencies and gives visitors an opportunity to explore how they can be involved in world mission. Christian Vocations produce a magazine with a list of current vacancies. Here's a sample from 2013:

- administrator (France)
- artist in residence (Middle East)
- Bible translator (Central Asia)
- business entrepreneur (Arab world)
- carpenter (Chad)
- community development facilitator (Africa)
- dancer and actor (Bosnia)
- dentist (Papua New Guinea)
- dorm parent (Zambia)
- football coach (Russia)
- IT consultant (Nepal)
- journalist (Austria)
- librarian (Tanzania)
- management advisor (Cambodia)
- mechanic (Guinea)
- science teacher (Tanzania)
- scriptwriter (Austria)
- speech therapist (Philippines)
- street children's worker (Uganda)

Whatever your skills, there's a need that you could meet if you have the right attitude and character.

Sometimes Christians have said (or acted as if) the spiritual is good or important while the material is bad or unimportant. In 1 Timothy 4 Paul calls this the 'doctrines of demons' (4:1 RSV). There were some in Ephesus where Timothy was working who denigrated sex and food. But Paul says that these things are good gifts from God. We can be spiritual people in marriage, in the home and so on. To be spiritual is to walk in step with the Spirit in every area of life, not to live on some ethereal plane. Salvation is not about escaping the prison of the body. Indeed, the gospel affirms that salvation involves the resurrection of the body. So Christians should be concerned with all of life and with whole people, body and soul.

If you're a parent, think about how you care for your children. More than anything, you want them to know Christ. So you tell them the gospel, teach them the Bible, involve them in your church, pray for them and model your faith to them. Given a choice, I would always choose for my daughters to be saved over having a good career. But it's not a choice I ever have to make. More than anything, I want them to be saved. But I still feed them, house them, clothe them and provide fun things for them to do! I care about their spiritual needs, but I also care about their physical, social and emotional needs.

In the same way, as we get to know people, we'll want them to know Jesus and find salvation in his name. But we'll also take an interest in their physical and social needs. We'll be committed to the whole person. Caring for someone also means caring about their family, community and nation, because this wider context shapes their lives for good or ill. Vinoth Ramachandra, the IFES Secretary for Dialogue and Social Engagement, told the Keswick Convention in 2000,

> When we read in the book of Revelation that . . . there will be no more pain and suffering, it challenges us now in the present to work to alleviate human suffering, to resist evil whatever form evil takes. And when we do that, whether in our local communities or on a global scale, we are pointing people to God's future. We are signs of his coming kingdom.[2]

Mission is love in action. Jesus not only gave us *the Great Commission* to make disciples. He also gave us *the Great Commandment* to love our neighbour. Gary Haugen, the former director of the UN genocide investigation in Rwanda, presents the case for broad understanding of mission in a simple but powerful way. He presents five heart-rending stories – all true cases taken up by the International Justice Mission of which he is president. Reflecting on the parable of the Good Samaritan, Haugen asks us to consider in each case: 'What does love require?'

Joyti is a 14-year-old girl from a rural town in India who was abducted and drugged by four women who sold her into a brothel in Bombay. She was locked away in an underground cell and severely beaten with metal rods, plastic pipe and electrical cords until submitting to provide sex to the customers. Now she must work seven days a week, servicing 20–40 customers a day.

Osner is a 45-year-old man in Haiti who was illegally arrested and thrown in prison when the local mayor wanted to seize part of his land for her personal use. The detention is completely illegal under Haitian law and five different court orders have been issued demanding his release, but the prison authorities refuse to release him because of their political relationship with the mayor.

Shama is a 10-year-old girl who was sold into bonded slavery for a family debt of $35, which was incurred to pay for her mother's medical treatment. As a result, for the last three years, Shama has been forced to work six days a week, 12–14 hours a day, rolling cigarettes by hand. She must roll 2,000 cigarettes a day or else she gets beaten. Her bonded slavery is completely illegal under Indian law, but local authorities do not enforce the law.

Domingo is an elderly peasant farmer in Honduras who was shot in the face and leg when police illegally opened fire on him and other Lenca Indians while they were marching in the capital city for better government services in their remote region. The President of Honduras issued a promise to compensate all the injured, but nearly a year has gone by and the payments have never come. Now Domingo has lost his house and land because he is disabled and cannot work to make the payments.

Catherine is a 13-year-old girl who lives in a Manila slum and cannot go to school because her aunt forces her to work as a domestic servant. Worse, Catherine's aunt allows some of her male friends to live in the house and one of them raped Catherine while everyone else was out of the home. Catherine managed to file a complaint with the police, but the rapist is the son of a policeman and they have ignored the order to arrest the man for two years.[3]

What does love require? What does it mean for us to love Joyti, Osner, Shama, Domingo and Catherine? Love certainly does require that the gospel is proclaimed to Joyti, to her oppressors and to her customers. But does that exhaust our obligation of love towards her? What does love require?

'Dear children, let us not love with words or speech but with actions and in truth' (1 John 3:18).

Mission embraces all of life. In a sense, mission is not simply an activity you do. It's not that you sign up to do some mission for a couple of hours each Saturday afternoon. For Christians, mission is an identity. In the power of the Spirit we live our whole lives for the glory of God as witnesses to Christ. So mission can include joining a fitness club, eating a meal with friends and watching a movie, *if* these things are done with missional intentionality.

Mission is everything, but proclamation is at the centre

There is a danger in saying that mission is everything, and that danger is that mission becomes nothing. It loses its gospel distinctiveness. People can be involved in mission in all sorts of ways. But central to mission must be the proclamation of Christ.[4] Mission is all about Christ, or it's not Christian mission!

Throughout the Bible our eternal future is said to matter more than our life in the present. Jesus says,

> Do not store up for yourselves treasures on earth, where moths and vermin destroy, and where thieves break in and steal. But store up for yourselves treasures in heaven, where moths and vermin do not destroy, and where thieves do not break in and steal.
> (Matthew 6:19–20)

Or again, in Luke 12:4–5 Jesus says,

> I tell you, my friends, do not be afraid of those who kill the body and after that can do no more. But I will show you whom you should fear: fear him who, after your body has been killed, has authority to throw you into hell.

Jesus isn't saying that our souls are more important than our bodies. His concern here is with our bodies. The point is that we shouldn't fear what people can do to our bodies in this life. We should instead be concerned about what God can do to our bodies in eternity. The issue is that our eternal fate is more important than what people may do to us in this life.

We see all sorts of needs around us. They are immediate and evident. But the priority of the eternal future means that the greatest need for all of us is to be reconciled to God and so to escape his wrath. And this is the greatest need of the poor.

This means it is never enough merely to address people's felt needs. Such needs can be a good starting point, as the gospel addresses the human condition in all its complexity. But we need to move beyond this. People rarely articulate God's judgment as a felt need. Indeed, people are blind to the need to escape God's judgment – the need which is in fact their greatest.

Without an awareness of eternal needs, our focus will over time become temporal needs, as these often demand our attention. We must consciously, therefore, keep in mind that greatest need which is known to us only through the gospel – that of a person to be reconciled with God and escape his wrath. This is usually the greatest challenge facing Christian social involvement, to keep in view the greatest gift we have to offer a needy world: the words of eternal life.

'I always try to have a parable up my sleeve.' That's how one missionary midwife working in North Africa put it to me. She went forward at the Keswick Convention to commit herself to world mission. Thirty-five years later she is still serving overseas, and she was visiting the Convention with the help of the Keswick Missionary Hospitality Fund. 'I try to be intentional about quoting Scripture into situations,' she explained. 'The Prodigal Son, for example, works well in a northern African village.' She was recently asked, 'Do you have a book with that in?', and so she was able to give the family a copy of the New Testament.

Putting proclamation and social action together

The proclamation and demonstration of the gospel go together. Think of it like this. One of the first rules for reading the Bible is to look at the context. If you want to understand a *text* (a word, a phrase, a paragraph or a story), you need to understand it in the light of its wider *context*. This is true of all 'texts'. Suppose I say, 'I'm mad about my car.' Does that mean I'm passionate about my car because I think it's wonderful? Or does it mean I'm angry because someone has just crashed into it? You can't tell just from the words on their own; it's the context that helps you to make sense of what I'm saying.

The same is true of the gospel message. The 'text' of this message is heard by people in a context. It's not a question of whether it should be or not. It always is. Our text, the message we proclaim, will be interpreted by the context of our lives and our life together as Christian communities. The question is whether that context matches the message of transforming grace in Jesus Christ. When the context of our lives doesn't match the text of our message, we shouldn't be surprised if evangelism becomes hard work. But when our message and our actions match, then people are more likely to be open to the gospel.

Paul tells Titus how he is to teach slaves to live 'so that in every way they will make the teaching about God our Saviour attractive' (Titus 2:10). Peter says, 'Live such good lives among the pagans that, though they accuse you of doing wrong, they may see your good deeds and glorify God on the day he visits us' (1 Peter 2:12). Jesus says, 'A new command I give you: love one another. As I have loved you, so you must love one another. By this everyone will know that you are my disciples, if you love one another' (John 13:34–35). In my experience people are often attracted to the Christian community before they are attracted to the Christian message. But their experience of Christian love then makes them interested in Jesus.

Reminding them of his ministry among them, Paul writes to the Thessalonians, 'Because we loved you so much, we were delighted to share with you not only the gospel of God but our lives as well' (1 Thessalonians 2:8). Some people engage in evangelism outside the context of a relationship (sharing the word without sharing their lives). Others never have the courage to share the gospel with their friends (sharing their lives without sharing the word). Paul shared both the gospel and his life with people – word and life together.

In 2007 Clive Calver told the Keswick Convention how he had visited a village in Mozambique with an African missionary called Linda Ngzane. The village treated him as royalty. But when he asked more, they said, 'It's not you really, it's Linda!' They explained, 'When she came, our children were dying.' The problem was diarrhoea and the false remedies of the witch doctors. Linda told them the witch doctors were wrong and offered a simple salt solution in the name of Jesus. When the children started to live, the witch doctors started to come to Christ. Calver was introduced to a parade of witch doctors who one after another spoke of how they had met Jesus and owned him as Lord and King.[5] This is the impact of a Christian sharing her life, together with sharing God's word.

8

Where? Everywhere with the
unreached as the priority

In the traditional image of mission, people go from the West to the non-Western world. The mission field is 'over there' somewhere. Whether it was ever appropriate to speak of the West as anything other than a mission field is questionable. But the secularization of the West means that we cannot avoid viewing our society as a mission field. Missiologist David Smith says, 'The culture-shock that I experienced [as a missionary] in West Africa over thirty years ago has now become familiar to Western church and mission leaders as they struggle to make sense of a context in which their organisations look increasingly like boats stranded by a retreating tide.'[1]

Mission is to everywhere

The reality is that the mission field is all around us. In 2011 Helen Roseveare told the Keswick Convention, 'Each of us is called by God and sent out to serve him. It doesn't matter how far he sends you – it might be to your next-door neighbour. Distance has got nothing to do with it.'[2]

One of the first people to alert us to this was Lesslie Newbigin. Newbigin was a missionary to India for many years. When he returned, he realized that the West was now a missionary context. There were still many individual Christians. But Christianity was no longer engaging with the culture. So Newbigin called for a missionary engagement with the culture.

In his book *Mission after Christendom*,[3] David Smith identifies three 'frontiers of mission'. A hundred years ago people would have assumed that the frontiers of mission were geographic. They were the places where the gospel was entering new territory. But Smith's frontiers are sociological:

- secularization
- pluralization
- globalization

Mission is to everywhere. It begins on our doorsteps and extends to the far corners of the world. But *the unreached must be our priority*. There are still around one billion people in the world who have not heard the message of Jesus.

The majority of these people live in the so-called '10/40 window', a term coined by the mission strategist Luis Bush. It refers to the regions of the world in the eastern hemisphere between 10 and 40 degrees north of the equator. This 'window' contains most of the unreached peoples of the world, as well as many of the world's poorest people. It is where most of the world's Muslims, Hindus and Buddhists live. Yet this region receives far fewer Christian resources and missionaries than elsewhere in the world.

Mission is from everywhere

As we have seen, the traditional image of mission involves

people going from the West. The West was the source of mission, while the rest of the world was seen as the recipient of mission. But this has changed rapidly. There are national and regional missionary movements springing up around the world, reflecting the shifting centre of gravity in global Christianity.

In his influential book *The Next Christendom,* Professor Philip Jenkins explores the implications of the rise of southern Christianity.[4] Jenkins charts how, over the past century, the centre of gravity of the Christian world has shifted to the south. Western Christianity may be declining, but it will be replaced not by Islam, he suggests, but by southern Christianity. The conflicts of the next century will not be between Islam and Western humanism, but between Islam and southern Christianity. Indeed, Jenkins questions whether the assumption that Christianity is a Western phenomenon has ever been true. He shows how Christianity has flourished outside Western empires. Even where Christianity has expanded under Western imperialism, Jenkins argues that its success cannot be explained in terms of fear or envy of the imperial conquerors. Christianity has genuinely taken root in indigenous local cultures. He cites the newer independent Christian churches in Africa as examples of this.

From its very earliest days, the Keswick Convention has welcomed many speakers from around the world, as it has tried to reflect the vitality of the global church. In 1897, for example, Samuel Crowther and Pandita Ramabai addressed the Convention.[5] Crowther was born in Nigeria under the name Ajayi. When he was twelve years old, he was captured by slave raiders and sold to Portuguese traders. But his slave ship was boarded by the British navy, and Crowther was taken to Sierra Leone. There Crowther was cared for by missionaries from the Church Missionary Society and he became a Christian.

He went on to become a church planter, Bible translator and bishop. He told the Convention about the self-supporting churches under his supervision in the Niger Delta.

Pandita Ramabai was an Indian social reformer who championed the rights of women. Her father was a Hindu Brahmin whose commitment to the education of women led to the social ostracization of their family. After her parents' deaths, Ramabai travelled all over India continuing her father's work. In 1883 she received a scholarship to train as a teacher in England, where she converted to Christ before returning to establish schools and continue her campaigning. At the Keswick Convention in 1897, 200 people responded to her call to serve in India.

The challenge of partnership

Imagine that someone from London comes to one of your Sunday services. None of you knows him. And he tells you that next Saturday morning he is going to give you all a seminar at a local hotel. He's going to tell you how you can do evangelism better by adopting an approach that's worked well in his homeland. What would you think?

This is not a far-fetched scenario. In fact, this sort of thing is happening around the world.

Recently I was in the Balkans with Brian Jose from Radstock Ministries. Brian could tell you many stories of people from the West turning up in the Balkans, expecting to 'do' mission for local churches. He asks them, 'Would you let an Albanian take over your meeting or programme if they turned up out of the blue?' And always they say, 'No'. But they can't see that that's just what they're doing! They assume they know best and that the Balkan church ought to be grateful for their help. Too often there is still a sort of paternal relationship in which

Balkan Christians are treated as children. They're not true partners in mission.

One of the major challenges facing mission in the future is the interface between southern and northern mission. This offers a wonderful opportunity for constructive partnership with mutual learning. Already models of mission are developing, of partnership with Western funding and technical skills facilitating non-Western organizations in mission. But money is a complicating factor in partnerships. The rhetoric of equal partnership is hard to sustain when money is involved. The reality is that 'he who pays the piper calls the tune'. The relationship between a rich Western church with declining numbers and a vibrant, growing, poor southern church will be a key issue in mission in the coming years.

Paul addresses this issue in Galatians. Some people in Galatia were teaching a message that, Paul says, 'pretends to be the Good News, but is not the Good News at all' (1:6–7 NLT). They are saying that Gentiles who have put their faith in Jesus *also* need to be circumcised. Paul's response is this: 'if you let yourselves be circumcised, Christ will be of no value to you at all' (5:2).

But there's another thing going on here. There's an underlying assumption in what the false teachers say. It's this: 'You Gentile Christians ought to listen to us Jewish Christians. You ought to do what we say. After all, our church in Jerusalem is larger, stronger, older, better resourced, more established. We have a long history stretching back to Abraham. The Good News came from us. We're your mother church. We're just being maternal. We want to look after our children.'

Think how that might sound today: 'You African or Asian Christians ought to listen to us British Christians. You ought to do what we say. After all, our church in Britain is larger, stronger, older, better resourced, more established. We have a long history stretching back to the Reformation. The Good News came from us. We're your mother church. We're just being maternal. We want to look after our converts.' No-one says it quite like that, but sometimes that's the subtext.

But Paul rejects this. He wants a partnership of equals. He wants partnership, not dependence. That's one of the central themes of Galatians. In Galatians 1:12 he says of his message, 'I did not receive it from any man, nor was I taught it; rather, I received it by revelation from Jesus Christ.' The gospel message is not from Jerusalem. It's not the property of the Jerusalem church. Nor the British church. The gospel did not originate with us.

This puts Paul in a dilemma because, as it happens, the leading figures in Jerusalem, the apostles, agree with Paul's position on circumcision. It would have been so easy for Paul to say, 'The big guns in Jerusalem are on my side, so listen to me.' If he had done that, then he might have won the circumcision argument, but he would have lost the equal-partners argument. He would have conceded that Gentile churches were under the authority of the Jerusalem church. And he won't do that. So we get this strange narrative in chapters 1 and 2: 'I met the apostles – but not straight away' (1:15–17). 'I met the apostles – but only a few of them' (1:18–19). 'They agreed with me – but their opinion doesn't really matter' (2:6, 9).

In Galatians 4:26 he says, 'Sarah . . . represents the heavenly Jerusalem. She is the free woman. And she is our mother' (NLT). Where is our mother church? Where is the church who gave us birth? Where is the church to whom we are accountable? Not in Jerusalem. Not in Britain. It's not the headquarters of a mission agency. Our mother church is in heaven. It is the congregation of people gathered around the throne of Jesus. So if we want to work with churches around the world, then we need to do so as equal partners.

It's not that the Western church has nothing to contribute. Clearly, it has much to contribute. We have a history, resources, understanding and people. But we must work with other churches as equal partners. They too have a history, resources, understanding and people. Indeed, when it comes to their context, they will usually have a better understanding. There are many things we can teach them. But there are also many things we can learn from them. Paul's goal is a partnership of equals.

Arnold Tucker was a pioneer of this kind of partnership. Tucker first felt called to mission at the Keswick Convention, and in 1890 he was sent by the Church Mission Society to be the Bishop of Eastern Equatorial Africa. Tucker was influenced by the great Victorian mission strategist, Henry Venn. Venn spoke about the 'euthanasia of missions', by which he meant that foreign missionaries should see themselves as temporary. They should convert and train local people who would then replace them. Together with Rufus Anderson of the American Board of Commissioners for Foreign Missions, Venn coined the term 'indigenous church'.[6] They said that missionaries should create churches that are self-supporting, self-governing and self-propagating (or in Venn's terms, 'self-extending').[7] Tucker shared these values, arguing that African churches should enjoy autonomy. His approach in Uganda had three phases: the conversion of individuals, the planting of churches and the education of leaders. He was also committed to adapting local cultures, rather than replacing them with European culture. The problem was, he argued, that too often we believe 'we have everything to give and nothing to receive; everything to teach and nothing to learn.' In 1911 he told the Keswick Convention how membership of the church in Uganda had grown from 200 to 70,000 during the thirty years he had been there.[8]

Those principles remain just as important today. At one Keswick Convention I met Edith Currie, a beneficiary of the Keswick Missionary Hospitality Fund. Edith spent over forty years in Africa. At the time she was teaching at the International Missionary College in Kenya, training east Africans for mission to unreached peoples, mostly in Kenya, but also generally throughout Africa. The college was established around three decades ago, and the current principal was one of the first students. What's more, the college currently has two Koreans training in Africa for Africa.

Much to give, much to receive

Let me summarize with two important principles.

First, mission is to everywhere, but the unreached must be our priority. Mission begins right on your doorstep. You're involved in mission every time you leave your home and whenever you spend time with unbelievers. There are needs all around the world. But our priority must be those who have not had the opportunity to hear the good news of salvation through Christ. Like Paul, it should be our 'ambition to preach the gospel where Christ was not known' (Romans 15:20).

Secondly, mission is from everywhere, but we in the West still have a role to play. The rise of the global church brings wonderful opportunities and some challenges, but it doesn't mean that our job is over. There are still many places where Christ is not known. We need humbly to learn to work alongside people from other nations, but we still need to work. We still have much to offer. *You* still have much to offer.

The task of world mission is becoming a global partnership. Perhaps today Bishop Tucker would say of us, 'We have much to give and much to receive; much to teach and much to learn.'

Part four:
The challenges of mission

9

The cultural challenge

Imagine an alien academic who visits Earth every few centuries to explore the phenomenon of Christianity. This is what the eminent missiologist Andrew Walls invites us to do.[1]

1. Jerusalem in AD 37

Our alien academic makes his first visit to Jerusalem in AD 37. All the Christians are Jews. They're meeting in the temple, offering animal sacrifices, marking the seventh day of the week, part of large families and reading old law books. They're seen as one denomination of Judaism, but they identify 'Messiah', 'Son of Man' and 'Suffering Servant' as Jesus of Nazareth.

2. The Council of Nicaea in AD 325

In AD 325 our alien returns to visit the Council of Nicaea. The participants come from all over the Mediterranean. Few are Jews, and in fact many are hostile to Jews. They're horrified by animal sacrifices and instead they offer bread and wine.

None is married, and indeed marriage is seen as a morally inferior state. They work on the seventh day of the week and meet on the first day. They read the same law books that were read in Jerusalem, but in translation. They also use works not written at the time of the first visit. 'Messiah' is just a surname for Jesus. More important are the names 'Son of God' and 'Lord'. They're debating the difference between the Greek words *homoousios* ('same substance') and *homoiousios* ('similar substance').

3. Ireland in the seventh century

In seventh-century Ireland our alien academic sees monks on a rocky coast. Some are standing in ice-cold water to pray. Others are leaving in small boats with illuminated manuscripts to call the inhabitants of Scotland to give up their nature deities. Others are hermits in dark caves. They all accept the findings of Nicaea, but their key debate concerns the date of Easter.

4. Exeter Hall, London, in the 1840s

A gathering listens to speeches promoting Christianity and commerce to Africa. They are organizing a deputation to the British Government to end the slave trade. Like the Irish monks, they talk of holiness, but they would be horrified at the suggestion that it means praying in icy water. Unlike the fasting monks, they're all remarkably well fed and active in all aspects of society.

5. Lagos, Nigeria, in the twenty-first century

A white-robed group is dancing and chanting through the streets. They're 'the Cherubim and Seraphim', and they are inviting people to experience the power of God in healing. They use the same book as that used by groups in previous visits. If asked, they would assent to Nicaea, but not with much interest. They're not politically active. They fast like the Irish monks, but only on fixed occasions.

All these groups are very different, and our extra-terrestrial scholar might doubt that there was even any connection between them. But each group self-consciously sees itself as part of the larger community to which the others belong.

Living between two homes

Wells makes sense of this diversity by arguing that there are two contrasting principles in Christianity:

1. The indigenizing principle
The gospel invites us to come to God as we are with all our cultural and social background. Throughout history Christians have tried to indigenize, to adapt the expression of their faith to their context. We make faith 'a place to feel at home'.[2]

Adoniram Judson, often called America's first missionary, for example, realized that the people of Burma were suspicious of Western church buildings. So in 1818 he built a *zayat*. A *zayat* was a shelter for travellers, which was also used by Buddhist monks for religious gatherings. Judson used his *zayat* to share the gospel and soon gathered a number of seekers who converted to Christ.

2. The pilgrim principle
But God not only accepts us as we are. He also changes us into what he wants us to be. 'Along with the indigenizing principle which makes his faith a place to feel at home, the Christian inherits the pilgrim principle, which whispers to him

that he has no abiding city and warns him that to be faithful to Christ will put him out of step with his society.'[3] No society has existed that can absorb the word of God painlessly. We are a pilgrim people heading towards a new homeland (Hebrews 11:8–16).

These two forces exist in tension: 'Just as the indigenizing principle, itself rooted in the gospel, associates the Christian with the *particulars* of their culture and group, the pilgrim principle, in tension with the indigenizing [principle], and equally of the gospel, by associating them with things and people outside the culture and group, is in some respect a *universalising* factor.'[4] 'Every Christian has dual nationality' – we have all the relationships with which we were brought up, plus the new relationships of the family of Christ.

This process was already at work within the New Testament, Wells argues. The Synoptic Gospels speak of Jesus in the terms he spoke of himself: 'the kingdom of God' and 'the work of the Son of Man'. But as Christianity moved into Hellenistic culture, new language was found to express the universal truth of Christianity, such as 'Word', 'Lord' and 'Pleroma' (fullness).

An understanding of culture

Culture is the air we breathe. It shapes our attitudes, speech, thinking, priorities, behaviour and relationships. Yet most of the time we are unaware of its influence. It is often the encounter with a different culture that first alerts us to many aspects of our own. To add to the confusion, we also need to recognize that cultures are always changing – especially through interaction with other cultures. This process of change is being accelerated by globalization. So if you want to understand a culture, you must know its history, but you must also recognize that it is changing.

Culture can be defined as *the rules (usually unwritten and often sub-conscious) that determine how people within social groups behave and think.* It's what makes you a stranger when you are away from home.

1. The rules

Social groups have their norms of behaviour. The problem is that these 'rules' are usually unwritten (though there may be some written elements like a national constitution or sporting rules) and often subconscious. As a result, cross-cultural inter-actions are like playing a game in which you don't know the rules. What's more, the people with whom you're playing often can't articulate the rules, but they always know when you've broken one! That is why people experience 'culture shock'. You become a learner, a child, a foreigner, an outsider.

2. Social groups

When we think of cross-cultural mission, we often think of reaching other ethnic groups. But all social groups have their own cultures, not just ethnic groups. Cultural groups can be defined by ethnicity, but also by social status (the working-class culture), occupation (the culture of the police, the culture of the medical profession), leisure activities (golf-club culture, hip-hop culture) and belief (evangelical culture). This means that cultures overlap. Any one person will be a participant in several cultures and subcultures – especially in urban areas where there is a greater mix. So any one person will be operating with several sets of unwritten, often subconscious, rules at the same time.

3. Behave and think

When we think about culture, we often start with behaviour and with actions that are considered polite or impolite, socially acceptable or unacceptable. These are the sorts of issues that surface quickly in cross-cultural encounters. But the issues of 'thinking' are often more significant. Consider the issue of self-esteem. In the West our identity is individual. If I am rejected or shamed, then I am crushed. My identity is determined by what happens to me. But in many non-Western cultures your identity is primarily communal or family. My identity is determined by what happens to my tribe or family. So if *I* am rejected or shamed, then I'm not completely crushed, because my identity is only partly shaped by what happens to me. But if my community is shamed, then my own sense of self is significantly affected. Or if my sister is rejected or shamed, then my identity is threatened. That's why Muslims in Pakistan can feel personally affronted by the American invasion of Iraq. That's why a British Pakistani family may reject a daughter who converts to Christianity.

You can understand how to *behave* in a polite way, but if you don't understand how people *think*, then your communication will often miss the mark. Imagine that you hear me say to my daughter, 'Let's meet at the normal time at the café where we met last week.' You know the meaning of every word in that sentence. But which café are we talking about and what's our normal time? To understand the message properly, you need to know something about the story and habits of our family.

The same is true when we communicate between different cultures. The obvious barrier to communication is language. But even if you know the language well, you will also need to understand the story and habits of the culture if you want to communicate effectively.

A Hindu may agree that Jesus is God. Under your influence he may start worshipping Jesus, and so you may regard him as a convert. But he may view Jesus as simply one god among many.

Case study: the excluded middle

The Christian anthropologist Paul Hiebert calls attention to what he calls 'the excluded middle'.[5] In Western cultures we tend to divide the world into two realms. The seen world is the world of science, sight and experience. The unseen world is the world of faith, God, religion and miracles. Even atheists recognize this division. But in many traditional societies around the world there is a middle category. They have a high God and the world of formal religion. But there is also a category in between, of ancestors and spirits, of shamans, magic and folk religion. Westerners frequently identify similarities and differences between the two cultures in the realms of the seen world and the high world, suggests Hiebert. But they often completely miss the significance of 'the excluded middle'. Development workers might install clean water, for example, but never address the traditional beliefs that prevent people from using the well. Or missionaries might reshape people's view of the seen world and the 'high' God, but never address the control that ancestor worship exerts. Later on they discover people are still attending local witch doctors because they've never discussed how the gospel impacts on belief in the spirit world.

Bryant Myers describes an exercise with a tribal group in India.[6] The group identified eight areas in which they would like to see social change. They were then asked to rank three possible sources of power over these areas: (1) the tribal group itself, (2) outsiders like the government, neighbours and development agencies, and (3) gods and spirits. In the minds of the villagers in seven of the eight areas, the gods and spirits exercised significant control. In every case the Western or Western-educated development workers ranked them as least significant.

Cultural generalizations can be helpful short cuts to understanding someone. But we also need to remember, first, that everyone is part of a common humanity. Whatever our differences, there are some things that are true of every human being. We are all, for example, made in God's image with a longing for relationships. We are all in rebellion against God, broken people who need salvation. So in every culture what people need most is the gospel.

Secondly, we need to remember that everyone is unique. Individuals within any culture will have aspects of their personality that are unique to them and which may contrast with their culture. We need to understand people on a person-by-person basis.

A biblical understanding of culture

God told humanity to fill the earth, and this has been commonly interpreted as including a mandate for cultural development and scientific endeavour. It was a call to create a variety of art and technology. God delights in the resulting cultural diversity. But as a result of human rebellion, every culture is now affected by sin. Individual actions and beliefs become engrained in culture and then shaped by that culture. Paul says, 'Do not conform to the pattern of this world, but be transformed by the renewing of your mind' (Romans 12:2). So all cultures are good, but fallen. They contain elements that accord with the gospel and elements that are confronted by the gospel. So Christians should celebrate and preserve local cultures while also being committed to the transformation of those aspects of the culture that are contrary to God's word.

The gospel itself transcends culture without denying cultural differences. It unites people of different races because what brings them together (Christ) is more important than what divides them (cultural diversity). We have a new identity in Christ that takes priority over our old identity (Luke 14:26). The church witnesses to the reconciling power of the cross (Ephesians 2:11–22) and the vision of people from every nation, tribe and tongue gathered around the throne of the Lamb (Revelation 7:9).

A missional understanding of culture

The reason why we want to understand a new culture is because we want to communicate the gospel to that culture. We want to adapt our methods and approaches so that we can effectively reach it. This is known as 'contextualization'. Paul describes his approach to contextualization in 1 Corinthians 9:19–23:

> Though I am free and belong to no one, I have made myself a slave to everyone, to win as many as possible. To the Jews I became like a Jew, to win the Jews. To those under the law I became like one under the law (though I myself am not under the law), so as to win those under the law. To those not having the law I became like one not having the law (though I am not free from God's law but am under Christ's law), so as to win those not having the law. To the weak I became weak, to win the weak. I have become all things to all people so that by all possible means I might save some. I do all this for the sake of the gospel, that I may share in its blessings.

Contextualization affects both our methods and our message. That doesn't mean we change the message of the gospel or water it down. Quite the opposite. Contextualization involves understanding the culture so that we can identify the 'bite point' – the moments where the gospel challenges the culture, offering good news and calling for repentance. Contextualization is not just about how we can be like the culture. It is also about identifying where the gospel is *different* from the culture. We need to understand a culture so that we can ensure that the challenge of faith and repentance are heard clearly.

Case study: the homogeneous unit principle

The missionary Donald McGavran became concerned about the lack of conversions seen by his mission agency. So he studied the factors that lead to church growth. His most controversial conclusion is that 'people become Christian fastest when the least change of race or clan is involved'.[7] Later he turned this observation into a principle: the so-called 'homogeneous unit principle'. Empirical evidence suggests, he argues, that 'people like to become Christians without crossing racial, linguistic or class barriers.'[8] As a result, homogeneous churches grow fastest. These are churches in which all the members are from a similar social, ethnic or cultural background. People prefer to associate with people like themselves, and so we should create homogeneous churches in order to be effective in reaching people.

The main criticism of the homogeneous unit principle is that it denies the reconciling nature of the gospel and the church. It weakens the demands of Christian discipleship and leaves the church vulnerable to partiality in ethnic or social conflict. It has been said that 'the homogeneous unit principle is fine in practice, but not in theory'!

Yet most churches are homogeneous to some extent. People choose churches on the basis of worship style, denominational allegiance, theological emphasis and even cultural background. As soon as you choose to operate in one language, you have created a homogeneous group. So some have argued that homogeneity is a good approach in mission, but people need to be introduced to the wider church with all its diversity. Unbelievers need to see the reconciling power of the cross and recognize the cultural repentance to which they are being called in the gospel. So within our church life we need to give expression to both cultural difference and unity in Christ. Precisely how this is done will vary in different situations.

Missionaries often identify bridges and barriers to the gospel. Bridges are behaviours, beliefs, attitudes and circumstances that offer opportunities for the gospel. An assumption that God exists is a bridge to the gospel, even if you then need to challenge the way people think about him. A sense of brokenness is often a bridge to the gospel, as people are willing to admit their need. Barriers are those things that make it difficult for people to connect with Christ. They will be different in every context, but might include things like prejudice towards the church, a suspicion of authority or a fear of standing out from the crowd. Identifying these barriers helps you to identify key messages that you'll need to emphasize if people are going to change. If fatalism is a barrier to the gospel, then you may decide repeatedly to emphasize the transforming power of God's Spirit.

Another way of thinking about this is to recognize that every culture has its own salvation stories, which have a way of making sense of life and suggesting where hope may be found. These stories map onto the Bible story:

- What gives people identity? = creation
- What's the problem? = the fall

- What's the solution? = redemption
- What are their hopes? = consummation

Each of these questions readily connects with the biblical story. Sometimes there will be resonance. More often there will be contrast. This exercise helps you speak the gospel into conversations. When you hear people talking about their identity, problems, solutions and hopes, you can connect these with the gospel story – either to affirm or confront the culture's stories.

Dan Strange, of Oak Hill College, London, suggests that we should see the gospel as 'subversive fulfilment' of all other religions and cultures.[9] Everyone has some knowledge of God. In Romans 1 Paul says, 'What may be known about God is plain to them, because God has made it plain to them' (verses 19–20). The problem is that in their pride and rebellion, people 'suppress the truth by their wickedness' (verse 18). Other religions and culture, suggests Strange, refashion divine revelation. They exchange the truth for distorted versions of the truth. They're both opposed to Christian truth and parasitic on Christian truth. So other religions and non-Christian cultures contain truth (because of general revelation and common grace), but they also twist and distort the truth. So there is both continuity and discontinuity between Christianity and other religions.[10] This means that the gospel both confronts alternative religious worldviews and offers appealing answers to the questions that other religions cannot themselves answer. Dan Strange calls this 'subversive fulfilment'. The gospel fulfils the deepest longings of a culture, but in a way that subverts and confronts some of its core allegiances.

The idea of 'subversive fulfilment' is a helpful way to think about a culture. What are the hopes, desires and longings in the culture? In what ways are they a distorted version of right hopes and right desires and right longings? This will show you both what repentance means for people and how the gospel is good news that fulfils their deepest longings.

A cultural understanding of ourselves

Clearly, we face the challenge of communicating the gospel to a culture. But also we are challenged by our engagement with another culture. We too are shaped by our culture with all its good and bad elements. Culture is so much part of who we are that often we don't notice its influence. We see other people's culture more clearly, because we see the contrast with our norms. But we need to recognize that these may be our cultural norms, not gospel norms. Our culture is not the standard from which other cultures deviate, nor the ideal to which other cultures should aspire.

The problem is that we are so immersed in our culture that we don't see it, let alone its defects. That is why *a missionary engagement with another culture is a two-way process*. Our culture starts to come into focus so that we can see it more clearly – good and bad – and the gospel can enlighten and transform it. Just as other people are shaped by their culture, so we too are shaped by our culture. We can easily read the Bible through the prism of our own culture. And because the ways of thinking within a culture are often subconscious, we may not realize the extent to which this is the case. It's often our inter-action with other cultures that reveals this. Our engagement with other cultures will expose our own cultural assumptions.

This can be very disconcerting. If some things are culturally relative, then why not all things? If some things I once accepted as givens turn out to be culturally conditioned, how can I be sure of anything? Can I trust the gospel, or is it too the product of a particular culture?

Andrew Kirk says, 'Perhaps the most effective check on a process of inculturation which is both fitting and proper' is *the universal church*.[11] He cites Las Newman from the Caribbean, who suggests that we should see the church as 'community in communion'. Both aspects are important. 'Community' expresses the mandate of the church to express the gospel to its particular culture. 'In communion' reminds us of the wider connections and common truth that bind each local expression of the gospel together.

But more than the universal church, the safeguard of truth is *the universal revelation* of God. The God of all nations has revealed himself to all nations. He has asserted his universal lordship over all peoples. He has revealed himself in an inculturated form, but his word functions as the foundation for Christian truth.

God revealed himself through the history and culture of Israel. He clothed his truth in culture. Ultimately, he revealed himself in a person – not a universal, abstract person, but a person who lived and spoke as part of a particular culture. 'The Word became flesh' (John 1:14). So we too need to be committed to clothing our proclamation with culture, engaging with culture, adapting to culture.

But before Christ is made flesh, he is the Word, the second person of the Trinity, God's self-revelation. John's Gospel begins, 'In the beginning was the Word, and the Word was with God, and the Word was God. He was with God in the beginning. Through him all things were made; without him nothing was made that has been made' (John 1:1–3). The word did not start from within one particular culture. It starts in heaven with God himself. It does not belong to one culture. Jesus is 'from heaven', as he reminds us, especially in John 3 and 6 (3:13, 27, 31; 6:31, 32, 33, 38, 41, 42, 50, 51, 58). The one God of all the earth communicates a message for all the earth.

And that message is that Christ is Lord of all the earth. So the word of God remains the touchstone of Christian belief. When Christians interact within cultures and across cultures, they can bring their discussions to the word.

Barclay Buxton went as a missionary to Japan in 1890. A few weeks after his arrival, over 700 people were attending his meetings, and within a year seven churches had been planted. Together with his co-worker Paget Wilkes, he founded the Japan Evangelistic Band, which, as we've already noted, was launched at the Keswick Convention in 1903.

Buxton placed great importance on learning the language. His son and biographer, Godfrey Buxton, comments,

> They knew that they would never be of real value if they could not preach fluently in Japanese and also follow up the conversation of anyone in distress or under conviction of sin. Many missionaries feel that it is enough to be able to give prepared addresses, and they hurry off to do so, with the result that their whole life service is on a merely superficial level.[12]

Buxton started wearing Japanese dress because it signified his association with the people. But Buxton also said, 'People talk much of the etiquette of Japan and the difficulty of learning it. I have found that love is all that is needed. If you love the people, your manners are not clumsy and, if they are different, the people will pass it over.'[13]

Even more remarkable for his time was Buxton's confidence in his converts and his readiness to hand on the work to them. Buxton started churches in homes, making the Japanese converts responsible for leading worship and encouraging them immediately to tell friends about Jesus. This led to spontaneous expansion. 'Missionaries went further afield to new pivotal positions, and Japanese took up responsibilities in the old and the new spheres. So there was a continual pressing out to new fields rather than a stationary work.'[14] The new believers were taught to trust the Holy Spirit and find answers to problems for themselves in the Bible. Buxton said the Holy Spirit was 'the only power for the conquest of Japan'.[15] 'The Japanese were encouraged to go forward beyond the control of the missionaries, and to press out in the first enthusiasm of their salvation, while yet receiving further definite Bible teaching.'[16] As he travelled, Buxton always took one or two converts with him so he could train them on the job. 'I feel that our best work here is preparing Japanese workers,' he wrote. 'If they get a clear understanding of the Bible, and a real revelation of Christ in their hearts, they can go out and do better work probably than we can.'[17] Soon Buxton was writing, 'Certain Japanese are already of a spiritual calibre that I feel it would be more suitable if I sat at their feet rather than they at mine.'[18]

The cultural challenge can sometimes feel overwhelming. But the word we proclaim is not a word from the West, but a word from God that transcends all the cultural varieties on earth. We can be confident that the gospel is 'the power of God that brings salvation to everyone who believes' (Romans 1:16). And, as Buxton reminds us, the Holy Spirit is working in and through us. And he is the Spirit of truth who speaks through God's word so that the word 'penetrates' through all our cultural difference to divide 'soul and spirit, joints and marrow' (Hebrews 4:12).

10

The personal challenge

'I've neglected the care and nurture of my soul. I'm on a sinking ship. Water is pouring into my vessel.'

'My soul feels like a spiritual, emotional and relational wasteland. My sense of God's love has vanished. How can I be an effective missionary in such a condition?'

These are quotes from serving missionaries cited by Paul Lindsay of Christian Vocations at the 2013 Keswick Convention. Missionaries are not the spiritual superheroes of the church.

I sat down with a missionary I was visiting in Central Asia. A team member was due to join them in a few months, and he'd asked me to provide some orientation for her before she left. So I asked him what he wanted me to cover. I expected he would major on some of the cultural challenges outlined in the previous chapter. But in fact it was all about the personal challenges she would face.

I've addressed this chapter to those serving as missionaries or considering missionary service. But it is just as important for those supporting missionaries to be aware of the challenges they face and how we can encourage them.

In 1 John 5:4 we read, 'This is the victory that has overcome the world, even our faith.' There are many practical solutions to the problems faced by missionaries. But the key to overcoming the challenge of mission is faith in God. It is the truth about God that enables people to persevere as missionaries.

Four liberating truths about God

1. God is gracious

When you first move to a new culture, most people are excited. You love your new life with all its difference and variety. But after a while those differences and the difficulties they present start to get you down. Then over time you begin to get the hang of your new situation and become culturally adept. You start to enjoy the fact that you can bridge two cultures. We can present this process in a diagram:[1]

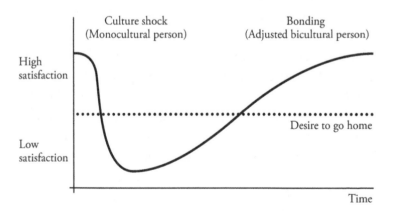

Mission agencies often advise new missionaries not to visit home during the first couple of years so that they get through this dip.

Think for a moment about what gives you a sense of achievement. A significant part of the problem is that when we first enter a new culture, all the normal things from which we gain a sense of worth, success, achievement and competence are stripped away:

- You'll feel incompetent to manage ordinary life. (Where do you buy glue? What do you say at a roadblock? How do you get your washing machine mended?)
- You'll be unable to communicate because of your lack of language ability.
- You'll be unable to relate because of your lack of cultural understanding.
- You'll be unable to do ministry or contribute to church life.
- You'll not achieve much because your work life is on hold for language learning.

All the things you use to justify yourself or the abilities you used to take pride in are taken away. Your behaviour will appear weird to people around you, and your productivity will be low.

It's not wrong to feel a sense of achievement in the areas above, as long as your ultimate identity in found in Christ. The test of that is when the sense of achievement is taken away. What remains? Where does your sense of worth reside? If you're moving to a new culture, then you are about to face that test!

Your true self will be revealed and exposed by the exhaustion of your routine, by the pressure of crises in church life and ministry and by the fatigue of continually relating cross-culturally. Your marriage may come under pressure because you'll have to cope with a different version of your partner and yourself. The pressures of cross-cultural life will reveal underlying attitudes and behaviours.

Jesus deals with these issues in Luke 10. In verses 17–20 the disciples return from a mission trip. They're excited because of all the success they've seen. Jesus shares their excitement. He says he has seen 'Satan fall like lightning from heaven' (verse 18). But he goes on to warn them: 'However, do not rejoice that the spirits submit to you, but rejoice that your names are written in heaven' (verse 20). Jesus himself then prays to his Father, rejoicing in his grace and rejoicing that the disciples are God's children (verses 21–24). Our sense of well-being should be based not on our success or failure in ministry, but on our identity in Christ.

Jesus goes on to tell them the story of the Good Samaritan (verses 25–37). According to Luke, Jesus tells this story because the teacher of the law 'wanted to justify himself'. This man wanted a checklist that he could tick off so that he could tell whether he'd made the grade. But, as the story reveals, we can't justify ourselves, for the task is without limit. How can we tick off the task of loving a needy world? Thinking about what you've *not* done is the root to madness. There'll always be more that could have been done. But if we've served Christ faithfully with our day, then we can be content.

More importantly, while we can never do enough to justify ourselves (as the teacher of the law wanted to do), we are justified freely by God's grace in Christ. We may never be able to finish the task of justifying ourselves, but his work is finished. He has made complete atonement for our sins. And in that there is rest.

The next story in Luke 10 is Jesus visiting the home of Martha and Mary. Again Martha wants to justify herself through her service. But Jesus says the necessary thing is to sit at the feet of Jesus and to listen to his teaching – to hear his word of grace.

So expect less productivity when you cross cultures. Expect cultural mistakes. Expect your sinful heart to be exposed. But when this happens, *find refuge in God*.

The Russian tennis player Vera Zvonareva was a finalist at Wimbledon in 2010. She had previously had a reputation for cracking on court. She would often be in tears, and her game would disintegrate. One of the techniques that she used to turn her career round was to put a towel over her head during breaks. She would block out the world around her and focus on what mattered.

We need to do the gospel equivalent. When you feel the pressure, block out the world – stop listening to its voice. Block out your own heart – stop listening to its doubts and desires. Instead, listen to the word of Jesus. Think of God's word as a towel you can put over your head for a few moments.

This is the truth that will set you free and get you through. Say to yourself,

- 'Therefore, there is now no condemnation for those who are in Christ Jesus' (Romans 8:1).

- 'See what great love the Father has lavished on us, that we should be called children of God!' (1 John 3:1).

- 'The Lord your God is with you,
      the Mighty Warrior who saves.
   He will take great delight in you,
      in his love he will no longer rebuke you,
   but will rejoice over you with singing.'
   (Zephaniah 3:17)

What do you want other people to see in you? When you're struggling, when you're having marriage difficulties, when you make mistakes, when you mess up? Will you want to hide this from people – from your team, from your unbelieving neighbours, from your supporters at home? What do you want other people to see in you? That you are a great person, or that you have a great Saviour?

2. God is glorious
If you're becoming a missionary, then you're going to be very conscious of what other people think about you.

Your fellow team members
Do fellow missionaries think you're competent? What are they making of your progress? How do they evaluate your ability to adapt to the culture? How do they evaluate your ability to adapt to the ministry? They'll be making a lot of suggestions, mostly from a desire to help. But to you, these may sound like criticisms – especially if you're already feeling insecure: 'You should have done this'; 'Don't say that'; 'You should try doing this.'

Your neighbours and friends
You want to make a good impression for Christ. What do your neighbours and friends think of you? What do they make of your strange ways? Are you getting the culture right? Are you reading their responses accurately?

Your supporters back home
People are giving sacrificially to support you. Are they getting value for money? Will they continue their support? Will they be impressed by your reports? Do they value what you're doing? What will you say when you have nothing to write

home about? What will you say when all you've been doing is slowly learning the language? What will supporters think when things go wrong? You will be going through experiences that are hard to share because they're outside other people's experience.

We can easily become controlled by the opinions of other people. This is one of the common reasons why we sin: we crave the approval of other people, or we fear their rejection. We 'need' the acceptance of others, and so we're controlled by them. The Bible's term for this is 'fear of man'. 'Fear of man will prove to be a snare,' says Proverbs 29:25, 'but whoever trusts in the LORD is kept safe.'

The Bible's response is a vision of the glory of God. We need a big view of him. We need to fear him. 'He will be the sure foundation for your times,' says Isaiah, 'a rich store of salvation and wisdom and knowledge; the fear of the LORD is the key to this treasure' (Isaiah 33:6). The key to God's treasure is to fear him. To fear him is to respect, worship, trust and submit to him. The fear of God is the natural response to his glory, greatness, holiness, power, splendour, beauty, grace, mercy and love. Often, in Psalms 18 and 34 for example, this is what the psalmist is doing. In the face of some threat, he is speaking the truth about God to himself. Keep telling your heart that God is glorious so that fear of others is replaced by trust in God:

> I sought the LORD, and he answered me;
>   he delivered me from all my fears.
> Those who look to him are radiant;
>   their faces are never covered with shame.
> (Psalm 34:4–5)

Again, think of putting that towel over your head so that you find refuge in God. Whenever you see someone you fear or whose approval you crave, imagine God next to them. Who's the bigger of the two? Who's the more majestic? Who's the holier? Who's the more beautiful? Who's the more threatening? Who's the more loving? It's an act of faith in God to open up and be able to say, 'I'm having a bad day. Please pray for me', instead of feeling the need to protect your reputation or project your best.

'Do not be afraid of those who kill the body but cannot kill the soul,' says Jesus. 'Rather, be afraid of the One who can destroy both soul and body in hell' (Matthew 10:28). The fear of God liberates us from being controlled by other people's expectations. We're controlled instead by God's expectations. We still serve other people. That's why we've been set free (Galatians 5:13). We take other people's expectations seriously because we want to love them as God commanded. But we're not enslaved by them, and we don't serve them for what they can give us in return (approval, affection, security). We serve them for Christ's sake. By submitting to his lordship, we're set free to serve others in love.

3. God is great

What are your worries about doing mission in another culture? The refrain we kept repeating when I visited missionaries in the Middle East was 'fallen world, sovereign God'.

This world is full of broken people, people who are sad, needy, insecure, people who misuse their power, people who are desperate to prove themselves, people who are fearful. And that's just your team! Seriously, your co-workers are fallen. Co-workers are the most common cause of grief on the mission field – perhaps because our expectations are higher. You too are fallen. You may be wondering, 'Will I be able to adapt? Will it get easier? Will I find friends?' Don't panic. It will come. You're not failing. You're normal. You're a frail, finite human being.

This world is fallen. It's a mess. It's full of corruption and injustice, full of lost people who desperately need a Saviour.

And you can't mend it. You're *not* sovereign and you're *not* infinite. If you try to fix everything, then you will burn out or break down. You can only do so much.

It's not just that there are some things you can't do. You can't do all the things you could do! In other words, there will be many things you could fix, but you'll lack the time or energy or emotional strength to address them. And that means there'll be many things that are left undone. Many suffering people unhelped. Many lost people who don't hear the gospel.

That can be difficult to live with. The danger is that it will drive you to overwork, overstress and overworry. Or you will push those emotions onto other people, making them feel guilty that they're not doing enough.

But here is the good news for you: God is great. He is sovereign. He's in control. He's the great mission strategist. He'll bring Christians into the lives of those he plans to save. You can trust him with the big picture. You're called to be *faithful* with the task which he gives to you and have *faith* in his sovereign control of the big picture.

Consider this: Jesus said, 'I have brought you glory on earth, by finishing the work you gave me to do' (John 17:4). Jesus could say that he'd completed the task. Yet after his ministry many people were left unhealed, many did not hear his proclamation, many were not fed. But he'd completed the task that God had assigned to him.

Give up any notion of being a superhero or a super-missionary. You can be mediocre! Forget your missionary hagiographies. This is not what you're called to be. You're called to be faithful, not fruitful. Keep telling your heart that *God is great*. He's in control.

Indeed, if you try to be a superhero, then you will distort the message. 'We have this treasure in jars of clay to show that this all-surpassing power is from God and not from us' (2 Corinthians 4:7). The message of the cross is proclaimed by weak people (1 Corinthians 1:18 – 2:5).

Your initial focus may be on learning the language. Don't have any bigger ambitions than this. Take a day at a time. Have small expectations for each day. Be patient. Be content with slow living. God will use you as he chooses if you're faithful to him.

God is also in control of the situation back home. You can trust God for those you've left behind.

4. *God is good*
What do you think you will miss most if and when you go on cross-cultural mission? Your answers might include: friends and family, home comforts, familiarity (e.g. favourite foods), entertainment options, a professional working environment, the Christian community, corporate worship and teaching.

What frustrations might you face? Your answers might include: the inability to operate in an unfamiliar culture, slow progress with language learning, conflict with colleagues, a lack of ministry opportunities, time-consuming, boring or annoying cultural customs, bureaucracy, inefficiency, corruption, injustice, setbacks and the special challenges and limitations on women in a patriarchal society.

All of these are real losses and real frustrations. As a result, it's all too easy to become bitter or resentful, or to despise the people you are reaching or the place where you live. It's not like home. They don't do things 'right'. They're resistant to your message. They don't enjoy the things you enjoy.

So work hard to enjoy your new neighbourhood and its culture. Sometimes this will be a choice. Make a habit of saying positive things about your city. Be 100 per cent there 100 per cent of the time. In other words, don't live in the past or the future, looking back or forward to life at 'home'. Make your home in the culture for as long as you are there.

Above all, choose to enjoy God. Keep telling your heart that *God is good*. Again, think of the towel over the head. Take refuge in God. Find joy in him. Get your pleasure from knowing him and being faithful to him. Remind yourself of all that he is and all that he has done. Search the Scriptures each day for something that makes you rejoice in God afresh.

As we saw in the Foreword, Helen Roseveare first heard the call to mission at the Keswick Convention and went on to spend twenty years in what is now called the Democratic Republic of Congo as a medical missionary. In 1964 she spent five months as a prisoner of rebel forces, during which time she endured beatings and rape. Speaking at the 2011 Keswick Convention, she said, 'There will be moments in all of our lives when it's tough . . . and if you ask, "Is it worth it?" you'll be tempted to say, "No". But if you lift up your hearts and your eyes to Jesus, fix your eyes on him as Hebrews tells us, you'll find that he'll never fail you, he'll never let you down, he is worthy.'[2]

The community of faith[3]

Discipleship is a community project. God has given us the Christian community so that we can challenge and comfort one another. The writer of Hebrews says,

> See to it, brothers and sisters, that none of you has a sinful, unbelieving heart that turns away from the living God. But

encourage one another daily, as long as it is called 'Today',
so that none of you may be hardened by sin's deceitfulness.
(Hebrews 3:12–13)

Day by day you'll need to remind one another of these truths so that your hearts do not become hardened.

These four liberating truths about God ('the four Gs') are a great resource as you encourage one another. They are a great way of 'speaking the truth in love' to one another (Ephesians 4:15). This is how we can help one another to fight sin. They're also a great diagnostic kit. When you face temptation or fall into sin, ask yourself, 'Which of these truths am I failing to embrace?'

1. God is gracious – so we don't have to prove ourselves.
2. God is glorious – so we don't have to fear others.
3. God is great – so we don't have to be in control.
4. God is good – so we don't have to look elsewhere.

These four truths also offer an alternative to legalism. People often try to change behaviour by providing a set of rules by which we should live. Legalism says, 'You should not do that.' But the gospel goes one better and thereby offers true hope. The gospel says, 'You need not do that because God is always bigger and better than sin.'

The four Gs bring *gospel* change because they offer good news. We're not simply telling one another off – that's legalism and it kills. The four Gs enable us to speak good news to one another:

• If I meet someone who is worried about life or is manipulative, then I can say, 'Here's good news – you don't have to be in control because God is in control.'

- If I meet someone who is enslaved by other people's opinions, who fears rejection or craves approval, then I can say, 'Here's good news – you don't have to fear others because God is glorious and he smiles upon you.'
- If I meet someone who is enslaved by the pursuit of wealth or pleasure or sex, I can say, 'Here's good news – you don't have to look elsewhere because God is good, and to know him is true joy.'
- If I meet someone who is desperate to prove themselves or make it in life or who looks down on others, I can say, 'Here's good news – you don't have to prove yourself because God is gracious and Christ has done it all.'

This doesn't mean it's easy. We're called to the fight of faith. During a visit to the Keswick Convention one year I climbed Skiddaw, the mountain to the north of Keswick, with a friend. It was hard work! The final push is across loose rock at a 45-degree angle. Each step is agony. Your calves are aching as you try to lift the weight of your body on tired legs. It feels like a form of torture. And this is what we do for leisure! So why do we do it? Why don't we just give up? Because we're confident that the view from the top will make all the effort seem worthwhile. And so it was for me and my friend.

This is a great picture of the way we're sanctified by faith. Sometimes it can be agony. Each step is hard work. It's painful. You feel like giving up or giving in. But you press on because faith tells you that the view from the top will be glorious. Legalism would make you climb the slope by berating you or beating you. And if you've ever tried climbing a mountain with reluctant children, you'll know that that approach doesn't work very well. At best, you might get them up one mountain, but you'll not get them up a second. The gospel gets you to the top of the mountain by promising you a glorious view from the summit. The path is no less hard, but there's a spring in your step as you anticipate what's coming. Faith is fixing your eyes on the mountain top. Every now and then you can turn round to get a glimpse of the glorious view, just as we experience more of God the more we know and serve him. And those glimpses are a foretaste of what's to come: the mountain top of God's eternal glory.

11

A big ambition and a big God

In the early nineteenth century, Europeans, including mission-aries, had begun to colonize the coast of southern Africa, but few had ventured inland. In 1834 David Livingstone heard the American missionary Robert Moffat call on his audience to reach 'the vast plain to the north' where he had 'sometimes seen, in the morning sun, the smoke of a thousand villages, where no missionary had ever been'.[1] Livingstone responded to that challenge, leaving for Africa in 1840 and becoming the first European to see the waterfalls he then named as the Victoria Falls. In 1856 Livingstone returned after sixteen years of service to a hero's welcome, and his account of his time in Africa became a best-seller.

Livingstone returned to Africa in 1865. As far as Europeans were concerned, he 'disappeared' into the heart of the continent for seven years until an American newspaper com-missioned H. M. Stanley to find him. When the two men finally met, there was a pause, which was broken by Stanley's now famous words, 'Dr Livingstone, I presume?' Less well known is the fact that Stanley urged the aged and infirm

Livingstone to return with him. He was, after all, now world famous and could receive treatment for his illnesses. But Livingstone declined. He remained committed to the task. He wrote in his journal, 'My Jesus, my king, my life, my all. Once more I dedicate my whole self to thee.'[2] A year or so later his African helpers found Livingstone dead, still kneeling by his bed where he'd been praying. His body was sent back to the UK where he was buried in Westminster Abbey. But, as he had requested, his heart was buried in Africa. He had lived and died fired by that vision of 'the smoke of a thousand villages, where no missionary had ever been'.[3]

Paul's ambition

It was that same kind of ambition that drove the apostle Paul. He says, 'It has always been my ambition to preach the gospel where Christ was not known, so that I would not be building on someone else's foundation' (Romans 15:20). Paul's ambition was to reach the unreached. It was an ambition not for his glory, but for the glory of Christ.

Paul's missionary letter

If Paul had set out to write a book on world mission for the Keswick Foundation series, what might it have looked like? I think the answer is that it would have looked like the letter to the Romans. Romans is Paul's defence of his mission to the nations. It's a support-raising letter. He wants the Romans to support his mission to Spain.

In Romans 1:9–13 Paul describes how he plans to visit the church in Rome. But he has in mind more than just a friendly visit with a bit of sightseeing: 'I am a debtor both to Greeks and non-Greeks, both to the wise and the foolish. That is why

I am so eager to preach the gospel also to you who are in Rome' (1:14–15). He wants to preach the gospel among them.

'I am a debtor,' says Paul, 'both to Greeks and non-Greeks.' Imagine that someone gave you £100 to give to me. You would owe a debt to me. Even though you hadn't borrowed the money from me in the first place, you'd owe me the £100. You'd have an obligation towards me. In the same way, God has given us the gospel to pass on to the nations. So we're in their debt. We owe them the gospel. We have an obligation to them – and to God – to proclaim the good news. This is why Paul wants to come to Rome.

But Paul's ambition is bigger than this. 'Through [Jesus Christ],' he says in 1:5, 'we received grace and apostleship to call all the Gentiles to the obedience that comes from faith for his name's sake.' As we've seen, the word 'Gentiles' in the Bible means 'nations' or 'peoples'. This is what Paul is about: mission to the nations. In chapter 15 he says,

> But now that there is no more place for me to work in these regions, and since I have been longing for many years to visit you, I plan to do so when I go to Spain. I hope to see you while passing through and that you will assist me on my journey there, after I have enjoyed your company for a while.
> (15:23–24)

Paul wants to make Rome a stepping-stone for a new mission to Spain.

That all sounds like fun, doesn't it? Or does it? What was life actually like when Paul came to visit? If you've read the book of Acts, you'll know the answer is this: trouble! Paul was controversial. He was controversial among Christians because he said Gentile converts didn't need to adopt a Jewish identity by being circumcised or keeping the Sabbath. And Paul was even more controversial among unbelievers. Everywhere he went, he attracted persecution. He gets arrested and mobbed and jailed and flogged. He's a magnet for trouble. So Paul coming for a visit wasn't necessarily good news! Do you really want this?

So Paul is writing to say, 'This is who I am. Don't believe the rumours. This is what I preach. This is my gospel.' The letter of Romans is a defence of Paul's mission to the nations and a defence of Paul's gospel for the nations. It's a missionary letter.

Compare how Romans ends with how it begins:

Romans 1:1–5	Romans 16:25–27
Paul . . . set apart for the *gospel* of God	in accordance with my *gospel*
regarding his Son . . . *Jesus Christ* our Lord	about *Jesus Christ*
through his *prophets* in the Holy Scriptures (literally '*writings*')	through the *prophetic writings*
all the Gentiles (or '*nations*')	all the Gentiles (or '*nations*')
to *the obedience that comes from faith*	to *the obedience that comes from faith*

The same big ideas are there at the beginning and at the end. And when that happens, you can be sure that those are going to be the big ideas all the way through. The book of Romans is about calling the nations to faith by proclaiming the gospel of Jesus Christ. It's all about mission. And Paul says this mission was promised beforehand in 'the prophetic writings' of the Old Testament. The Christian life is all about mission because the Bible is all about mission. Paul is saying, 'Mission is not just my personal version of Christianity or my specialist interest – this is the Bible story.'

So in the letter of Romans Paul revisits the Bible story in the light of what Jesus has done. He tells the story of creation (chapter 1), of Adam as humanity's representative (chapter 5), of humanity's fall into sin (chapter 1), of Abraham's calling (chapter 4), of Israel's calling (chapters 2, 9 – 11), of the exodus (chapter 6), of the giving of the law at Mount Sinai (chapter 7), of God leading Israel through the wilderness into a new inheritance (chapter 8). Paul is showing how Jesus fulfils the Old Testament, *with the result* that people from all nations can become part of God's people through faith in Jesus without having to become Jewish or follow the Jewish law.

Paul was controversial because people thought he was inventing this new idea of Gentile mission. But the letter to the Romans is Paul saying, 'No, this was always the plan. Mission is not some trendy idea. It's the climax of the Bible story.' Think about it: the stories of Abraham and Moses and David and the prophets come to their climax *in your church* as people from the nations come to the obedience of faith.

A big ambition

That's *the logic* of the letter. But its heartbeat, its passion, *its ambition* is proclaiming Christ where Christ is not known. That's what Paul says in Romans 15:20: 'It has always been my ambition to preach the gospel where Christ was not known.' Reading Romans should give us the same ambition as Paul: an ambition to preach the gospel where Christ is not known.

At one Keswick Convention I met a Brazilian couple who were beneficiaries of the Keswick Missionary Hospitality Fund. Three years after his conversion, the husband was reading Romans 15:20 and he prayed, 'I want to do this. Show me what to do.' A short time later he was invited to a mission-ary conference. What he didn't know was that the theme was on the need to reach Muslims. He took this as an answer to his prayer. He went on to spend ten years working with Muslims in Brazil before he and his family went to the Middle East for two years to learn Arabic. They then felt God calling him to reach Muslims in a city in the UK. But they were worried because it was expensive and they feared that their church in Brazil might suspect they were after a comfortable life. But meanwhile the church was feeling called by God to send people to Europe. So now, fully supported by his Brazilian church, they are reaching Muslims in the UK.

We need to own the task of reaching the unreached. Millions of people have not heard the gospel. Large parts of the world are without a church. According to Wycliffe Bible Translators, 350 million people don't have even part of the Bible in their language.

We can make a difference. We may not be able to reach a billion people, but we can still reach some. And we can reach people who will reach others. We already have thousands of potential partners across the world. So we should be able to say with real meaning, 'We're committed to the task of reaching the unreached.' We can look round the world and say, 'This is our job.'

But what can we do? How can you and I reach the world? Isn't that a crazy idea? And what can we do when things look bleak or when we face setbacks?

In Romans 4 God quite literally promises the world! 'It was not through the law that Abraham and his offspring received the promise that he would be heir of the world, but through the righteousness that comes by faith' (verse 13).

Who are these heirs who will inherit the world? The answer is: people from many nations:

The promise comes by faith, so that it may be by grace and may be guaranteed to all Abraham's offspring – not only to those who are of the law but also to those who have the faith of Abraham. He is the father of us all. As it is written: 'I have made you a father of many nations.'
(verses 16–17)

Or again in verse 18 Paul says this promise is for 'many nations'. God's promise is that people from *many nations* will be heirs of his new world. Salvation will come to *many nations*. Churches will be planted in *many nations*.

One of the fun things that often happen at the beginning of a Keswick Convention week is that delegates are invited to say where they're from. It quickly becomes apparent that many nations are represented. There's often a competition to see who's come the furthest. These moments are a sign that God is at work fulfilling his promise.

God's great grace

But you may be saying, 'Me, a missionary? Reaching unreached lands? Translating the Bible? Planting churches? Are you crazy? I'm not that kind of super-Christian! I'm just an ordinary Christian. I'm not good enough for that kind of thing.'

Look at how Paul says that God will fulfil his promise of reaching the nations: 'It was not through the law that Abraham and his offspring received the promise that he would be heir of the world, but through the righteousness that comes by faith' (verse 13). We don't receive God's promises because we're good people who keep his law. We receive God's promises through faith, through Jesus.

What is it that qualifies us to receive God's promise? 'The promise comes by faith, so that it may be by grace' (verse 16).

'By faith' is shorthand for 'by faith in the work of Jesus'. Jesus has done all that's required to qualify us to be heirs of the world. He bears the judgment we deserve, and we receive the reward he deserves. He takes our sin, and we receive his righteousness. 'The promise comes by faith, so that it may be *by grace.*'

But also 'the promise comes by faith so that it . . . *may be guaranteed.*' If salvation is based on law or on our goodness, then there could be no guarantee. Maybe today you'll have a good day. But what about tomorrow? The promise would be like sand running through our fingers. But because it's based on faith in what *Jesus* has done, it's guaranteed, because the work of Jesus is guaranteed. Stamped on the work of Jesus is: 'lifetime guarantee' or '*eternal* lifetime guarantee'.

But, remember, what is the promise? It's not just that I can be right with God (though it certainly includes that). The promise is much bigger than that. God promises Abraham 'the nations'. It's the promise that many nations will be part of God's people. This letter of Romans is an invitation to partner with Paul in planting churches in Spain. Paul reminds them of the promise because he's recruiting!

Has God given us the task of world mission because we're deserving? Did God say to himself, 'Tim Chester – I must have him on my side!'? No, God's grace doesn't just guarantee our salvation; *grace guarantees our witness*. We don't need to be perfect Christians in perfect churches or part of perfect missionary teams. Imagine if the world needed Christians who perfectly kept the law. There would be no witness! But we're witnesses *to grace*. It is true that grace *is* transforming – our love and our life are going to be different because we point to a power beyond ourselves. But even when we fail, our lives are a witness *if* we have faith in Jesus and confidence in grace. We're witnesses not to *our* good works, but to the good work of Jesus.

Do you know what they sing in heaven? Revelation 5:9–10 says,

> You are worthy to take the scroll
> and to open its seals,
> because you were slain,
> and with your blood you purchased for God
> persons from every tribe and language and people
> and nation.
> You have made them to be a kingdom and priests to
> serve our God,
> and they will reign on the earth.

Who has won the lost? Who has purchased people from every nation? Jesus. Jesus has done the hard work of world mission through his blood. But notice too that Jesus makes us a kingdom and priests. It's an allusion to Israel's calling to be a royal priesthood who made God known to the nations. We don't become missionaries by doing mission. We become missionaries *through the cross*, and that then is why we do mission.

So the promise of many nations *depends on God's grace, not our goodness*.

God's great power

It is not just God's grace that sustains Paul's vision for the nations, but also God's power. Paul goes on in Romans 4, 'As it is written: "I have made you a father of many nations." [Abraham] is our father in the sight of God, in whom he believed – the God who gives life to the dead and calls into being things that were not' (verse 17). Paul says two things about God. First, God gives life to the dead. Secondly, God calls into being things that were not. That's a reference to creation out of nothing. There was nothing, and then God spoke, and this world came into being out of nothing.

It's the same with God's work of *re*creation. Right from the beginning it has depended on God's power rather than our abilities. When God first chose Abraham, it looked like he'd made a crazy mistake. Abraham couldn't become the father of one person, let alone many nations! Abraham's body 'was as good as dead', and Sarah's womb 'was also dead' (verses 18–19). But Abraham did become the father of many nations. From the beginning, God's people were a miracle. The first child born into God's family was born to an old, barren couple. From the beginning it was clear: the promise *depends on God's power, not our abilities*.

We will reach the nations through God's power. It has been the same all the way through the story. That's because at the heart of the story are the cross and resurrection of Jesus. The Old Testament prophets spoke of a faithful remnant among God's people, the true people of God. But in the story the faithful people came down to one person: Jesus. And then he hung on the cross. He breathed his last. And there was no-one left. The people of God were dead. But on the third day Jesus rose again. He burst from the grave, and we walked out with him. This is the foundational event for God's people: Jesus Christ bursting from the tomb. He's our life and our hope. He's the promise of all nations:

> The words 'it was credited to him' were written not for him alone, but also for us, to whom God will credit righteousness – for us who believe in him who raised Jesus our Lord from the dead. He was delivered over to death for our sins and was raised to life for our justification.
>
> (Romans 4:23–25)

God creates his people through the resurrection of Jesus. That's the defining event in our story. That's the foundation. It all rests on that moment.

But that's also the pattern repeated again and again in world mission. God 'gives life to the dead and calls into being things that were not' (verse 17). When things seem dead or nothing is happening, God can bring life because he 'gives life to the dead and calls into being things that were not'.

Jesus uses a very striking image in John 12:24–26. He invites us to imagine a seed. A seed in a packet does nothing. It just sits there, doing nothing, achieving nothing. But if you let it fall, if it dies (as it were) and you bury it in the ground, then it produces a harvest. Jesus is talking about his own death. Like a seed, he will die. But through his death there'll be a harvest of life from all nations. But then he says that anyone who serves him must follow him. This is the pattern for all his followers. If we give up our lives to him, if we die to ourselves, then we will produce a harvest. In 1996 Charles Price told the Keswick Convention,

> Some of us don't want any cost. We want a deluxe, first-class ride to heaven. I tell you, you won't know the blessing of God – not in the way you might know it if you were to say, 'Lord, Your will be done . . .' I'm inviting you to offer your body without reserve to Jesus Christ, in a way you never have before; to obey His call, His instructions, His will for your life. What he's going to do with it is His business.[4]

Back in 1905 Sister Eva of Friedenshort told a meeting for women at Keswick how she had disposed of all her possessions to serve Christ. The only things she still had were a ring and a clasp, which she'd kept for sentimental reasons. But now the Lord was impressing upon her afresh the needs of the lost, and so she laid them on the table at the front. One after another, women followed her example and put jewellery, watches and coins on the table.[5]

In 2 Corinthians 4:11–12 Paul says, 'For we who are alive are always being given over to death for Jesus' sake, so that his life may also be revealed in our mortal body. So then, death is at work in us, but life is at work in you.' Behind every lively church, every living Christian, every missionary advance is someone who is dying, someone in whom death is at work, someone dying to self. But in the mission of God, death always leads to life.

How will we fulfil the task of world mission? Through dying to self and through resurrection power. In 1933 people at the Keswick Convention were invited to ask themselves, 'What am I going to do with my life? That is the challenge. Am I going to lay it on the altar of self? Or am I going to lay it upon the altar of God's service and leave it there?'[6]

Again and again in church history, setbacks have proved to be advances. Failures have led to greater success. People have been martyred, and through their deaths many have come to know Christ. Others have died to self – giving up careers, wealth, comfort – and through their sacrifice life has come to others.

When I worked for Tearfund, one of our partners was involved with a church in Sudan whose building was bull-dozed. The result? Four new churches sprang up across the neighbourhood.

During the 1970s President Mengistu in Ethiopia imple-mented what was called the Red Terror. One and a half million people died and church buildings were closed down. When Mengistu fell, no-one was sure what would remain of the church. But Christians had been meeting secretly in homes, and the church had not only survived, but grown.

Often the persecutors of the church are like people blowing apart the head of a dandelion. All you're left with is a bare, empty stalk. Except that dandelion seeds are scattered, and up come new dandelions. That's not a good idea if you want a perfect lawn. But it's good news if you want to spread the fame of Jesus.

Here's the key thing: *God didn't 'find' a faithful people – he created them from nothing; he brought them back from the dead.* God doesn't tour the world looking for the best people he can find. Mission is not God recruiting the brightest and best for his cause. Don't ever think, 'God is fortunate to have me on his side.' God can call into being things that are not. He can take dead stones and make them sing his praises.

We've seen that God will reach the nations through his grace, and we've seen that God will reach the nations through his power. *God's grace plus God's power equals God's glory.* Abraham 'did not waver through unbelief regarding the promise of God, but was strengthened in his faith and gave glory to God' (Romans 4:20). Abraham gave glory to God. When things looked hopeless, Abraham still believed God had the power to do what he had promised, and that brought glory to God.

'We have this treasure in jars of clay to show that this all-surpassing power is from God and not from us' (2 Corinthians 4:7). The treasure is the gospel message we proclaim. The jars of clay are ordinary Christians like you and me. Ordinary Christians proclaim Christ, and the result is that lives are changed. It's an act of God's power that leads to God's glory.

We can have big ambitions because we have a big God. As one of my heroes, William Carey, perhaps the father of the modern missionary movement, famously said, 'Expect great things from God; attempt great things for God.'

Notes

Preface

1. John Piper, *Let the Nations Be Glad! The Supremacy of God in Missions*, 3rd edn (IVP/Baker, 2010), p. 15.
2. Joshua Project, a ministry of the US Centre for World Mission: www.joshuaproject.net.
3. Helen Roseveare, *Living Faith: Willing to Be Stirred as a Pot of Paint* (Christian Focus, 2007), p. 31.
4. W. H. Aldis, *The Keswick Week 1947* (Marshall, Morgan & Scott, 1947), p. 15.

1. In the love of the Father

1. Gottfried Osei-Mensah, 'The Helper from Heaven', in *God's Very Own People*, Keswick Year Book 1984 (STL, 1984), p. 165.
2. B. Godfrey Buxton, *The Reward of Faith in the Life of Barclay F. Buxton* (Japan Evangelistic Band, 1949), p. 185.
3. Samuel Zwemer, *Thinking Missions with Christ* (Marshall, Morgan & Scott, 1934), p. 67.
4. Samuel Zwemer, 'Calvinism and the Missionary Enterprise', *Theology Today* 7:2 (1950), p. 208.

5. Cited in Walter B. Sloan, *These Sixty Years: The Story of the Keswick Convention* (Pickering & Inglis, 1935), p. 85. Zwemer used the word 'Mohammedan' instead of the word 'Islamic'.

2. In the name of the Son

1. Adapted from an address given at the Keswick Convention in 2011.
2. Chris Wright, in *Word to the World*, Keswick Year Book 2011 (Authentic, 2011), p. 19.
3. Ibid., p. 25.
4. Hymn by Isaac Watts, first published in *Hymns and Spiritual Songs* in 1709.
5. Wright, *Word to the World*, p. 25.

3. In the power of the Spirit

1. Adapted from an address given at the Keswick Convention in 2011.
2. Walter B. Sloan, *These Sixty Years: The Story of the Keswick Convention* (Pickering & Inglis, 1935), p. 44.
3. Philip Hacking, *What He Says, Where He Sends* (Marshall Pickering, 1988), p. 69.
4. David Shibley, *Great for God: Missionaries Who Changed the World* (New Leaf Press, 2012), p. 46.
5. Ibid., p. 47.
6. Cited in Shibley, *Great for God*, pp. 47–48.
7. Peter Maiden, 'Preaching the Word', in *The Glory of the Gospel*, Keswick Year Book 2005 (Authentic, 2005), p. 151.

4. A promise for the nations

1. Philip Hacking, *What He Says, Where He Sends* (Marshall Pickering, 1988), p. 21.
2. Ibid., p. 22.

3. Ibid., p. 24.
4. Ibid., p. 24.

5. The hope of the nations

1. Jangkholam Haokip, 'Christian Mission and Kuki Identity', June 2013, www.bethesda.org.in/indigenous-resources/ article/christian-mission-and-kuki-identity. See also Joelouis L. Songate, 'A Little Known Quarryman in Wales', *The Evangelical Magazine*, 26 April 2010, http://magazine.emw. org.uk/2010/04/a-little-known-quarryman, and Rochunga Pudaite, *The Book That Set My People Free* (Tyndale House, 1982). For more information on Lamboi's own ministry, see www.bethesda.org.in.
2. Cited in Jay Reenders, 'The Book That Set My People Free', http://reformedandbiblical.blogspot.co.uk/2013/02/the-book-that-set-my-people-free.html.

6. Who? Everyone with the church at its heart

1. John, email to author, 10 August 2013. I have omitted John's surname because of the sensitive nature of his current work.
2. George Verwer, 'The Christian Service Meeting: Senders and Goers', in David Porter (ed.), *New Beginning, Old Paths*, Keswick Year Book 1987 (STL Books, 1987), p. 220.
3. John, email to author, 10 August 2013.
4. Gavin Reid, 'Christ's Commitment and Ours', in David Porter (ed.), *New Beginnings, Old Paths* (STL, 1987), pp. 209–210.
5. Jason Mandryk, *Operation World: The Definitive Prayer Guide to Every Nation*, 7th edn (Biblica, 2010; www.operationworld.org).
6. Bill Wilson, 'Seven Ways to Pray for Your Missionary' (OMF, 1998; www.omf.org/omf/uk/resources/ideas_for_prayer/ seven_ways_to_pray_for_your_missionary).

7. What? Everything with proclamation at the centre

1. Ruth and Vishal Mangalwadi, *Carey, Christ and Cultural Transformation: The Life and Influence of William Carey* (OM, 1993), pp. 1–8.
2. Vinoth Ramachandra, 'Radical Living', in Hilary Price (ed.), *One Lord, One Church, One Task*, Keswick Year Book 2000 (OM, 2000), p. 217.
3. Gary A. Haugen, 'Integral Mission and Advocacy', in Tim Chester (ed.), *Justice, Mercy and Humility: Integral Mission and the Poor* (Paternoster, 2002), p. 189.
4. For more on this, see Tim Chester, *Good News to the Poor* (IVP, 2004).
5. Clive Calver, 'Grace for the World', in *Unshackled? Living in Outrageous Grace*, Keswick Year Book 2007 (Authentic, 2007), p. 211.

8. Where? Everywhere with the unreached as the priority

1. David Smith, *Mission after Christendom* (DLT, 2003), p. xii.
2. Helen Roseveare, in *Word to the World*, Keswick Year Book 2011 (Authentic, 2011), p. 51.
3. David Smith, *Mission after Christendom* (DLT, 2003).
4. Philip Jenkins, *The Next Christendom: The Coming of Global Christianity* (OUP, 2002).
5. Walter B. Sloan, *These Sixty Years: The Story of the Keswick Convention* (Pickering & Inglis, 1935), pp. 48–50.
6. Wilbert R. Shenk, 'Henry Venn's Legacy', *Occasional Bulletin of Missionary Research* 1:2, 1977, 16–19.
7. John Mark Terry, 'Indigenous Churches', in A. Scott Moreau (ed.), *Evangelical Dictionary of World Missions* (Baker, 2000), pp. 483–485.
8. Walter B. Sloan, *These Sixty Years: The Story of the Keswick Convention* (Pickering & Inglis, 1935), p. 68.

9. The cultural challenge

1. Andrew F. Walls, *The Missionary Movement in Christian History: Studies in the Transmission of Faith* (Orbis, 1996), pp. 3–7.
2. Ibid., pp. 7–8, 53–54.
3. Ibid., p. 8.
4. Ibid., p. 9.
5. Paul Hiebert, *Anthropological Reflections on Missiological Issues* (Baker, 1994).
6. Bryant Myers, *Walking with the Poor*, revd edn (Orbis, 2011), pp. 280–281.
7. Donald A. McGavran and C. Peter Wagner, *Understanding Church Growth* (Eerdmans, 1970; 3rd edn 1990), p. 165.
8. Ibid., p. 163.
9. Gavin D'Costa, Paul F. Knitter and Daniel Strange, *Only One Way? Three Christian Responses to the Uniqueness of Christ in a Religiously Pluralist World* (SCM, 2011), p. 93.
10. Ibid., p. 114.
11. Andrew Kirk, *What Is Mission?* (DLT, 1999), p. 93.
12. B. Godfrey Buxton, *The Reward of Faith in the Life of Barclay F. Buxton* (Japan Evangelistic Band, 1949), p. 60.
13. Cited in ibid., p. 62.
14. Ibid., p. 77.
15. Cited in ibid., p. 61.
16. Ibid., pp. 78, 126.
17. Cited in ibid., p. 75.
18. Cited in ibid., p. 110.

10. The personal challenge

1. Adapted from Paul Hiebert, *Anthropological Insights for Missionaries* (Baker, 1985), p. 65.
2. Helen Roseveare, in *Word to the World*, Keswick Year Book 2011 (Authentic, 2011), p. 51.

3. For more on this, see chapter 3 of Tim Chester and Steve Timmis, *Everyday Church* (IVP, 2011).

11. A big ambition and a big God

1. David Shibley, *Great for God: Missionaries Who Changed the World* (New Leaf Press, 2012), p. 62.

2. Ibid., p. 64.

3. Ibid., p. 64.

4. Charles Price, in *Clean Hands*, Keswick Year Book 1996 (OM, 1996), p. 170.

5. Walter B. Sloan, *These Sixty Years: The Story of the Keswick Convention* (Pickering & Inglis, 1935), p. 60.

6. Ibid., p. 105.

KESWICK MINISTRIES

Our purpose

Keswick Ministries is committed to the spiritual renewal
of God's people for his mission in the world.

God's purpose is to bring his blessing to all the nations
of the world. That promise of blessing, which touches
every aspect of human life, is ultimately fulfilled through
the life, death, resurrection, ascension and future return of
Christ. All of the people of God are called to participate in
his missionary purposes, wherever he may place them. The
central vision of Keswick Ministries is to see the people of
God equipped, encouraged and refreshed to fulfil that
calling, directed and guided by God's Word in the power
of his Spirit, for the glory of his Son.

Our priorities: Keswick Ministries seeks to serve the local
church through:

- **Hearing God's Word**: the Scriptures are the foundation
  for the church's life, growth and mission, and Keswick
  Ministries is committed to preach and teach God's Word
  in a way that is faithful to Scripture and relevant to
  Christians of all ages and backgrounds.
- **Becoming like God's Son**: from its earliest days the
  Keswick movement has encouraged Christians to live
  godly lives in the power of the Spirit, to grow in Christ-
  likeness and to live under his lordship in every area of
  life. This is God's will for his people in every culture
  and generation.
- **Serving God's mission**: the authentic response to
  God's Word is obedience to his mission, and the
  inevitable result of Christ-likeness is sacrificial service.

Keswick Ministries seeks to encourage committed discipleship in family life, work and society, and energetic engagement in the cause of world mission.

Our ministry

- **Keswick: the event**. Every summer the town of Keswick hosts a three-week Convention, which attracts some 15,000 Christians from the UK and around the world. The event provides Bible teaching for all ages, vibrant worship, a sense of unity across generations and denominations, and an inspirational call to serve Christ in the world. It caters for children of all ages and has a strong youth and young adult programme. And it all takes place in the beautiful Lake District – a perfect setting for rest, recreation and refreshment.
- **Keswick: the movement**. For 140 years the work of Keswick has impacted churches worldwide, and today the movement is underway throughout the UK, as well as in many parts of Europe, Asia, North America, Australia, Africa and the Caribbean. Keswick Ministries is committed to strengthen the network in the UK and beyond, through prayer, news, pioneering and cooperative activity.
- **Keswick resources**. Keswick Ministries is producing a growing range of books and booklets based on the core foundations of Christian life and mission. It makes Bible teaching available through free access to mp3 downloads, and the sale of DVDs and CDs. It broadcasts online through Clayton TV and annual BBC Radio 4 services. In addition to the summer Convention, Keswick Ministries is hoping to develop other teaching and training events in the coming years.

Our unity

The Keswick movement worldwide has adopted a key Pauline statement to describe its gospel inclusivity: 'for you are all one in Christ Jesus' (Galatians 3:28). Keswick Ministries works with evangelicals from a wide variety of church backgrounds, on the understanding that they share a commitment to the essential truths of the Christian faith as set out in our statement of belief.

Our contact details

Mail: Keswick Ministries, Rawnsley Centre, Main Street, Keswick, CA12 5NP, England
T: 017687 80075
E: info@keswickministries.org
W: https://keswickministries.org

Related titles from IVP

KESWICK STUDY GUIDE

Sent
Serving God's Mission
Tim Chester

ISBN: 978–1–78359–654–6
80 pages, paperback

By tracing the origins of mission right back to God's character, and then seeing how it unfolds throughout the storyline of the Bible, we begin to understand how important it is to him.

As we see his heart for mission and the nations, we are challenged to discover God's plan for us too. Will this change our priorities as individuals and churches? Dare we see our place in God's plan and own the task of reaching the unreached?

Available from your local Christian bookshop or **www.ivpbooks.com**

Related titles from IVP

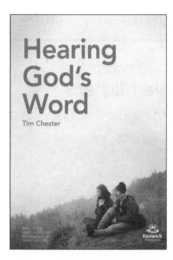

KESWICK STUDY GUIDE

Hearing God's Word
Tim Chester

ISBN: 978-1-78359-581-5
80 pages, paperback

What has God said? How has he said it? And how does it apply to our lives today?

Hearing God's Word invites us to explore these questions and more.

Each session starts with an introduction to the topic and then moves to a Bible passage. We focus on the theme, go deeper and explore living out the word in our daily life. Useful prayer prompts also help to make the message real and personal.

Praise:

'Biblical, practical, devotional and thoughtful. An excellent resource for group or personal study to strengthen our convictions about the truth of the Bible, and enable us to discover its riches for ourselves.' **John Risbridger**

'Here is a workable, practical guide that will help you to study the Bible by yourself or with others. Used well, it will help you grow in your faith.' **Ian Coffey**

Available from your local Christian bookshop or **www.ivpbooks.com**

Related titles from IVP

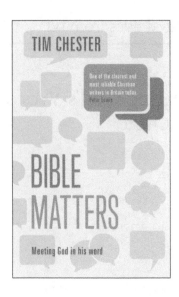

KESWICK FOUNDATIONS

Bible Matters
Meeting God in his Word
Tim Chester

ISBN: 978–1–78359–579–2

176 pages, paperback

Of course the Bible matters. It is God's word to us. But how do we engage with its message?

Tim Chester creates a sense of expectation, causing our reading of the Bible to become a living experience in which we encounter God. Amazingly, this God of the universe speaks to us each day!

Here is a personal, clear, intentional and sufficient message for our lives. The Bible is truly unique; it speaks into myriad situations and brings us back to the deep joy of the gospel.

Praise:

'Will enrich your encounter with God as you engage with his word.' **Elaine Duncan**

'This is more than useful; it's inspiring.' **Julian Hardyman**

'Tim Chester is one of the clearest, most useful and reliable Christian writers in the UK today . . . He comes alongside the reader to instruct and to apply his teaching to life in the modern world.' **Peter Lewis**